Teams in Library Technical Services

Edited by
Rosann Bazirjian
Rebecca Mugridge

The Scarecrow Press, Inc.
Lanham, Maryland • Toronto • Oxford
2006

SCARECROW PRESS, INC.

Published in the United States of America
by Scarecrow Press, Inc.
A wholly owned subsidiary of
The Rowman & Littlefield Publishing Group, Inc.
4501 Forbes Boulevard, Suite 200, Lanham, Maryland 20706
www.scarecrowpress.com

PO Box 317
Oxford
OX2 9RU, UK

British Library Cataloguing in Publication Information Available

Library of Congress Cataloging-in-Publication Data

Teams in library technical services / edited by Rosann Bazirjian, Rebecca Mugridge.
   p. cm.
 Includes bibliographical references.
 ISBN-13: 978-0-8108-5294-5 (pbk. : alk. paper)
 ISBN-10: 0-8108-5294-2
 1. Team librarianship—United States. 2. Technical services (Libraries)—United States. 3. Academic libraries—United States—Administration—Case studies. I. Bazirjian, Rosann. II. Mugridge, Rebecca, 1963–
 Z678.T43 2006
 025'.02—dc22

                          2005031326

♾™ The paper used in this publication meets the minimum requirements of American National Standard for Information Sciences—Permanence of Paper for Printed Library Materials, ANSI/NISO Z39.48-1992.
Manufactured in the United States of America.

Contents

Introduction

During the past fifteen years, self-directed work teams have become quite common as a way of organizing administrative units in library technical services operations. After the team phenomenon hit the business world, it made its way quickly to nonprofit organizations, including universities and libraries. Technical services, with its focus on productivity and a need to collaborate with other library units, seemed to be a logical place to apply team concepts. The research and case studies described in this book show the reader that teams came into being in many organizations for a variety of reasons, from budget and staffing concerns to issues about productivity and throughput. Technical services' need to be flexible and easily adaptable to meet new challenges, apply new and changing cataloging rules, address various workflows, process new types of materials, and so on made it a natural place to apply team concepts.

PURPOSE AND SCOPE

Teams in Library Technical Services is intended for managers and other librarians who are interested in the history of teams in library technical services units, the application of team theory, and the assessment of team organizational structure in libraries. Its emphasis is on the organization and assessment of teams, managing teams, and types of teams, primarily in academic libraries. Themes that reoccur throughout are the relationships between professional and support staff, the changing roles of librarians, and how managers and teams address issues such as performance evaluation, rewards and recognition, hiring, workload and workflow, and process improvements.

Assessment of team organizational structures is a prominent theme in this book. Many of the authors report on an assessment process of the effectiveness of team structure at their respective libraries, with several of them making some organizational changes to address weaknesses or needs, but keeping the team structure, and one of them returning to a more hierarchical structure. Two authors report on their libraries' return to a more hierarchical structure based on administrative preferences, rather than an assessment of team structure.

ORGANIZATION

This book is organized into four parts. The first part addresses teams from a theoretical or historical perspective. Jack Montgomery provides an excellent introduction to the concept of teams in library technical services in a chapter that addresses the role of organizational culture and how it impacts teamwork. Michael Norman provides an overview of team applications in library technical services in a discussion of teams at the University of Arizona, the University of New Mexico, Pennsylvania State University, the University of Kentucky, the University of California, Irvine, and the University of Illinois. In the last case Norman includes an in-depth case-study analysis of the team structure and effectiveness. In the third chapter in this part, Michael Ray provides a case-study approach to the development and impact of teams at the University of Arizona, well known for its implementation of teams across the library, not just in technical services.

The second part addresses four libraries' attempts to evaluate the effectiveness of existing teams. M. Sue Baughman, Gordana Ruth, and Janet Siar report on the University of Maryland's program review in 2000–2001, intended to assess the implementation of teams that had been formed three years earlier. Sarah Shreeves, Stephanie Hartman, and Elke Piontek-Ma discuss the factors that contributed to the long-term success of a team in the Massachusetts Institute of

Technology Libraries. Marda Johnson approaches the team history and organization at the University of Arizona in a more granular fashion, looking at the three work teams in their Technical Services and Archival Processing Team. Finally, Paul Orkiszewski, Megan Johnson, and Eleanor Cook discuss the evaluation of team training at Appalachian State University. Each of these assessments resulted in making some changes to one or more aspects of the team but maintaining a team organization.

The third part addresses three libraries' respective evaluations of the team organization but with the result that the team organization was discarded and the units returned to a more hierarchical organizational structure. Robert Alan reports on his assessment of the Pennsylvania State University Serials Department's team structure and the return to a more hierarchical structure with a supervisor in charge of the two serials acquisitions teams. John Lubans Jr. reports on his experiences working with team organizations at Duke University, highlighting the successes that were achieved during a period in which employees were empowered and workflows were streamlined. In the third chapter in this part, Mary McLaren reports on the return to a more traditional management structure at the University of Kentucky after eight years of self-directed work teams.

The final part of the book includes two chapters that address specific types of teams. Robert Freeborn and Ann Dodd report on a short-lived process improvement team organized to address a series of specific problems that had been identified regarding the technical processing of video materials at Pennsylvania State University. Michele Crump then discusses the use of matrix teams at the University of Florida. Matrix teams can be cross-functional and cut across departmental lines, allowing them to be more functional and less reliant on the chain of command for decision making.

We hope that *Teams in Library Technical Services* will prove a useful resource for managers and administrators who are contemplating a move toward teams or reviewing the effectiveness of teams at their own institutions. One of the themes that stands out in this collection is the need for ongoing assessment of the effectiveness of teams. It's critical to maintain an openness and flexibility regarding organizational structure, and an ongoing review of that structure and its effectiveness allows libraries to make ongoing organizational corrections that improve or enhance the capabilities of technical services units.

Part 1

THEORETICAL/HISTORICAL
PERSPECTIVE ON TEAMS

Chapter 1

The Role of Organizational Culture in Effective Team Development

Jack G. Montgomery

The concepts surrounding team management and organizational culture may seem unrelated when the implementation of some form of team management is initially considered; however, in fact the concepts are intimately connected. The success of any team management effort may depend on the successful identification, understanding, and management of that wide variety of social and procedural elements collectively known as the organizational culture. This chapter examines the role of organizational culture and how it impacts a manager or administrator introducing and implementing team management concepts to the workplace. The author examines the definition of organizational culture and the various types of cultures and also suggests ways to operate within an organizational culture and successfully implement a team management program within one's culture.

SO WHAT IS AN ORGANIZATIONAL CULTURE AND WHY DOES THIS MATTER TO TEAMWORK?

The concept of organizational culture, like that of team management, may be somewhat new to many librarians and unwelcome to many who have traditionally viewed themselves as removed from the competitive atmosphere of the for-profit sector of our society and therefore immune to the factors that influence the business world. As a consequence, librarians and library administrators have developed and maintained a limited if not naive perception of how our institutions were socially configured and managed. Fortunately, those sorts of ideas and attitudes are quickly fading from view, like those of the card catalog and the practice of guttering. In his chapter titled "Culture and Leadership in Universities" William Taylor states that "current political and economic pressures and constraints upon universities are forcing a move from a person-oriented to a role and power-oriented culture."[1] Today enlightened library administrators are actively seeking to learn the science of management and help their organizations evolve into the modern, dynamic institutions they are capable of becoming. A major part of learning to administer an organization consists of correctly observing, identifying, and understanding the character and personality of the organization. Understanding an organizational culture is essential to identifying the complex and often esoteric dynamics and features of a workplace. Such understanding is clearly essential for a manager to make any attempt to bring change or new ideas such as the concept of team management into a group. An administrator or even a manager must make certain that the organizational culture is capable of being receptive to the innovations that are being considered. "The wrong culture can sabotage vision, sandbag goals, and undermine values," writes author William Umiker.[2]

SO WHAT IS AN ORGANIZATIONAL CULTURE AND HOW DOES IT FUNCTION?

William Sannwald, in his article "Understanding Organizational Culture," defines four key functions of an organizational culture as follows:

- An organizational culture conveys a sense of identity to those who work within it and to those who come into contact with it. In addition, "it conveys to staff what is unique about the organization and what sets it apart from other organizations."[3]
- An organizational culture instills a sense of value and purpose to what takes place as a result of the organization's activity, and "it provides collective commitment to the organization."[4]
- An organizational culture promotes a "system stability, which is the extent to which the work environment is perceived to be positive and reinforcing."[5]

- It provides a rationale for the workplace and "allows people to make sense of the organization."[6] This understanding helps those involved in the culture to identify and develop the goals and objectives necessary to proceed in a logical and productive manner.

In one sense, a healthy organizational culture is analogous to the healthy personality of an individual. A healthy person must have a clear sense of self, established ethics and values, a sense of purpose and self-control, and a reason for being; hence, an organizational culture is the collective personality of an organization and must embody those same attributes. Most of us do not develop as individuals as a result of a clear and distinct written agenda but evolve gradually as a result of contact with a host of different circumstances, situations, and people. Each of these factors leaves its mark on our individual psyches, and while the source may be forgotten, the effects continue to manifest themselves in our future. As a result, like an individual personality, there are often complex and hidden elements that have evolved unconsciously over time and may be operating without the person's awareness. All of these elements exist in spite of a person's education, social standing, or ethnicity, and may lead to contradictory and nonproductive reactions. The same scenario exists for any organizational culture. An organizational culture may have developed historically in a manner that is totally out of sync with the formal written description of the culture often found in mission statements, organizational charts, or job descriptions. It is, therefore, essential for an administrator or manager to identify and understand the actual cultural elements at play. Understanding the particular culture of an organization, however, is not an absolute guarantee of success in implementing and managing cultural innovation or change. Sannwald reminds us that "even with the best intentions, skills, and cooperation, new supervisors sometimes fail in a culture. The primary reason is tied to their people skills."[7] A manager or administrator may not even personally fit the culture in which he or she is attempting to function; however, understanding one's organizational culture is an excellent place to begin. In this way, potential obstacles to team management may be identified and possibly modified before actual implementation is attempted. Tata and Prasad found that "work-teams change the way people interact and work in organizations. The implementation of teams is context-dependent, the success of which can depend on the alignment between team-level and organizational-level structural factors."[8]

DIFFERENT STYLES OF ORGANIZATIONAL CULTURE

There are many descriptions and models for organizational cultures available in the popular literature of business to help a person identify what defines a particular culture. In their book *The Character of a Corporation* Rob Goffee and Gareth Jones define four styles of organizational culture: *communal, fragmented, networked,* and *mercenary.*[9] They offer a series of diagnostic tools to help pinpoint which culture exists in a given place and time. To make an accurate identification of an organizational culture, the researcher should pay careful attention to factors such as how the physical elements of the work environment are structured, how and by whom communication is structured, how communication flows within the organization, how work time is managed, how people accomplish tasks, and how people identify themselves as individual working entities within the different parts of the organization. This identification process involves a considerable as well as an ongoing time investment on the part of the supervisor, but the rewards are immense in terms of one's eventual success. The researcher must also be aware that this attempt to examine, analyze, and interpret the existing organizational culture may be viewed by others as threatening and potentially subversive by others in that culture. William Taylor asserts that often within existing organizational cultures,

> Official descriptions are, in formal doctrine, isomorphic with the organization itself. Description is tolerated within limits. Analysis, comparison, interpretation, evaluation and explanation are more threatening. Mapping features of the organization onto other systems deprives it of uniqueness. The reductionism involved in analysis robs it of dignity. Potentially at least, comparison and evaluation can undermine the authority and status of its leaders. The alternative accounts offered by interpretation and explanation weaken the power of the official ideology.[10]

These statements should not, however, dissuade the researcher but alert him or her to the delicate nature of this undertaking and the need for administrative support for the effort as well as careful attention to the diplomatic elements required.

Four Types of Organizational Cultures

The following entries are Goffee and Jones's descriptions of the four basic types of organizational cultures commonly found in business and industry. No culture is considered better than any other, and there are both positive and negative features and expressions associated with each type. Each culture, however, does create and disseminate many overt and subtle messages that are internalized by everyone involved and, in turn, form the basis of that particular culture.

The Communal Culture

Goffee and Jones identify communal culture as having an overriding communal paradigm that combines the competitive spirit often associated with a mercenary culture with the work ethic of the networked culture. Communal cultures have an interest in results yet are concerned with process and with people. There is distinct focus on high sociability with a strong, almost religious sense of commitment on the part of managers and workers alike. Often communal cultures mold themselves around a single person or group of persons and their particular vision of the work and institutional mission. Goffee and Jones use the example of a start-up company focused on a single product or goal. Such a company would be highly focused on the success of that product or goal and hence embody some elements of the mercenary culture to be mentioned later. They've observed that many organizations with mercenary cultures may also have communal cultures within them.[11]

Friendship and kindness are personal and cultural traits valued in a communal culture but only as they relate to the mission or goal of the culture, which is internalized and followed with an almost religious level of commitment. The institution may openly refer to itself as "a family." In this culture, an employee or manager walks the walk and talks the talk 24/7 as a way of embodying the cultural ideals. All of this can, in a negative sense, take a heavy toll on one's life outside work. It can also be devastating should those occupying the exalted positions fail in some manner. Also, if employees do not appear to buy into this vision or offer criticism, they are usually seen as traitors. Employees in communal cultures are often expected to attend company parties and other social events designed to strengthen the group. Employees not totally committed to the communal ideals may resent this constant intrusion into their personal lives. An example of communal culture is embodied in the Japanese business work ethic and communal culture that requires workers to go out with their colleagues almost every evening to engage in elaborate socials designed to build solidarity.

Goffee and Jones suggest that a communal culture can exist for a time in an organization before possibly evolving into another type of culture. A library might adopt a communal culture during the initial stages of its organizational development and then change to a networked culture as the organization matures. Those individuals involved both emotionally and cognitively in communal culture often feel empowered as individuals and as an organization by and as a result of the high level of personal commitment required to make it functional. Such a focus can also make employee discipline and evaluations a very difficult, unpleasant process, yet such a process is also necessary to retain the solidarity.[12] The close-knit communal culture requires that all people depend upon their immediate colleagues for just about everything and envision their first loyalty always to the organization. This dynamic can lead to a lack of self-examination and unwillingness to offer critiques of the culture or its practices even when prudence dictates so, and failure to self-critique can lead to disaster.

The Fragmented Culture

In a fragmented organizational culture, a low value is placed on the collective experience and a high value on individualism and autonomy. Employees are expected to be "free agents," distinct individuals with highly developed specific skills who function in an almost autonomous manner with regard to their work. This type of culture exists in fast-paced, high-risk organizations, such as investment banking, advertising, and in some high-technology fields, as well as within academic departments and faculty in universities. Goffee and Jones define this type of organizational culture as having "low sociability and low solidarity."[13] They also state that people in a fragmented culture "work at an organization but for themselves."[14] While many librarians would not recognize themselves as working in a fragmented culture, Goffee and Jones suggest it is a very common culture in educational and academic-based institutions where "your standing is also built on the outside world's assessment."[15] Within the traditional academic fields, a scholar gains status and prestige based on his or her professional development and intellectual output. The concept of bonding with or loyalty to a group of colleagues or even the institution is a distant second to being valued by your subject-based peer network. Most fragmented cultures have a certain disdain for any sort of group or team project or cooperative efforts. As a result, trying to implement traditional team management structure in such a culture is going to be difficult at best, if not impossible, without a significant change in the culture itself. Organizing the fragmented organizational culture along the concepts of team management could be akin to herding cats.

In a fragmented culture, even simple attendance at meetings and planning sessions is often considered a disdainful obligation rather than something of value. Leadership roles in this type of culture, such as that of an academic dean, may be viewed as an unwelcome, imposed assignment. In an odd twist of fate, many academic library organizations, which have a traditional service relationship to their university faculty, may unconsciously adopt the same fragmented culture posture and even in some cases develop a certain disdain for the service aspect of their profession. Clearly this form of cultural mimicry is usually going to be counterproductive to the organizational health of the library.

Results from a recent survey published in ALA Editions, *Managing Conflict in Library Organizations: Strategies for a Positive Productive Workplace*,[16] seem to indicate that academic librarians have the greatest difficulty with positive self-image due to the predominance of fragmented cultures in library cultures in the halls of academia. However, as Goffee and Jones indicate, such a culture honors "ideas, not individuals," and people may be hired for their intellect rather than their ability to get along and work well with others.[17]

These trends applied to the academic hiring process have created a managerial system in higher education that is often ineffective and organizationally dysfunctional. It may reflect the classic scenario of a cognitively brilliant individual who is hired for research and teaching but who later is "promoted" to a position of administrative responsibility. Such individuals are often asked to manage a culture that they barely comprehend and often do not appreciate. Ironically, the skills such scholars were prized for go to waste as they struggle to master a bureaucratic maze of university regulations and rules that seem meaningless compared to the important intellectual work to which they long to return. What usually lures rank and file professors to such choices is the extra "battle pay" that department head and other administrative positions include.

Goffee and Jones note that fragmented cultures can produce impressive results. They also advise managers to be alert for the negative expressions of fragmentation, "where low solidarity and low sociability are creating dysfunctional organizational outcomes. Other warning signs: pervasive cynicism, closed doors, difficulty in recruiting, and excessive critiquing of others. In other words, ideas may matter, but so do the people promoting them, and no one is safe."[18]

Not surprisingly, any of the above warning signs could be found in an academic library. It is critical to the future of academic librarianship that there exist a balance between the university's culture and the internal culture of the library. Librarians in higher education should strive to avoid adoption of the negative features of the fragmented culture often promoted by their colleagues in the academic departments. Emulating the culture of the parent institution, in this instance, is likely to create a damaging environment. Academic librarians need to consider deliberately what cultural values prove most effective for their situation as a part of the larger institution and educational process so as to retain the ideals of service in their professional lives.

The Networked Culture

A networked culture is characterized by the fact that "people know and like each other—they make friends, as the rule goes, all over the organization."[19] Networked cultures, like communal cultures, often foster high levels of socialization between their members, which can foster a high degree of loyalty and commitment to the organization and its goals. Significant value is placed on the ideal of reciprocity in human interactions, and a "we all look after each other" attitude is present. Such organizations often have an emphasis on ease of communication and acceptance of individual expression and value the interconnected, interdependent nature of their work-related activities. Individual differences are downplayed as unimportant. Due to this recognition of the collective value system of communication and expression, decisions tend to take longer than in some other models, but the degree of support for those decisions is often higher. Goffee and Jones suggest that in the networked culture great value is placed on helping others in a selfless manner. This sometimes expresses itself well during organizational strain with other departments. People's willingness to pitch in to assist when needed, or even "helping before they are asked," is evident.[20] This organizational atmosphere allows the institution to respond quickly and effectively to changes in the workplace. The networked culture, as a result, is a fluid, adaptable organizational culture. As Riane Eisler states in her article on the concept of partnership as a managerial ideal, "Already, there are calls in the organizational change literature for a recognition that we are interdependent on rather than independent of one another."[21] Many libraries may have networked cultures as their primary culture or embedded within a larger culture. Many technical services departments develop as networked cultures due to the interrelated, interconnected nature of the finished product. On the other hand, many public services departments, especially in academic environments, develop as fragmented cultures due to a wide variety of educational experiences and backgrounds and the independent nature of the services they deliver.

Such an environment may have some qualities that seem ideal, especially for a service-oriented business like a library, but it is certainly not for everyone. Some people are not accustomed to a high degree of sociability and may not feel comfortable in a networked culture. Similarly, individuals brought up with and rewarded for displaying a high degree of competitiveness may find the "let's all work for each other" atmosphere frustrating. These individuals need the excitement of competition to spur them to achievement. This need is not necessarily a personal flaw, but the networked culture is simply not a place where such a person can find satisfaction.

The Mercenary Culture

On the flip side of the networked culture is the mercenary culture, a culture most organizations have, at least at certain times. Mercenary culture is "restless and ruthless" and includes the "hallmarks of high solidarity: strong, rather fierce, agreement around goals, a zest to get things done quickly, a powerful shared sense of purpose, a razor-sharp focus on goals and a certain boldness and courage about overcoming conflict and accepting the need to change."[22]

Goffee and Jones admit that in a positive sense the mercenary culture can be highly productive. Results and success are prized above all else. Employees are encouraged to compete, yet they work together to overwhelm any outside competition. This effort can take on the quality of a military campaign. Perceived adversaries may become problematic for a mercenary culture unless management clearly and continuously identifies the enemy in some productive fashion. A mercenary culture also will be in the throes of constant analysis and evaluation so as to retain its place "on the hill."

Mercenary cultures are also goal-driven cultures in which one campaign follows another in a military-like atmosphere. Being traditionally service oriented, relatively few libraries are mercenary in nature. They nevertheless have had a taste of the mercenary atmosphere as a result of rapid technological changes foisted upon them over the past thirty years. As soon as librarians recover from one wave of techno-fads and management innovation, another one comes along right behind it. Library administrators may compete with each other to see who can show off the trendiest innovations first, or the most radical ideas in organizing their staff, or who can dream up the most unique new service. This atmosphere can readily catapult library organizations from one type of culture to another. A library with a cooperative, networked culture may find itself radically transformed into a mercenary culture as a new innovation, major staff change, or organizational shift takes place. For example, if cross-functional "teams" are formed where before there had been hierarchical departments, confusion and dysfunction may last several years before people get used to the new ways of interacting. Budgetary shortfalls or increases will shift a culture if one group must compete with another for scarce or new resources. During such times, the level of networking and human interaction radically drops off as the competition intensifies. To many of the formerly networked people in the organization, this phase often seems like a world turned upside down; resistance takes on an intensity that matches the intensity of the change.

In a positive vein, if properly managed, the mercenary culture can shift the organization without damage to accomplish a short-term goal that has been clearly identified and had the groundwork established. As with managing change, managing an organizational shift, either temporarily or permanently, should be carefully planned, with the vision for change being clearly stated and passionately promoted throughout all chains of command on an ongoing basis throughout the process. This culture must be monitored and adjusted so that the momentum and energy of the organization is turned toward the objectives rather than drained away in subversion and resistance.

The intense focus on results and success in a mercenary culture invariably leads to a situation of "winners and losers." In short, if an individual fails to perform, the results and penalties are swift. Goffee and Jones point out that a "mercenary culture's low sociability also brings with it a certain attractive ethos of fairness. Because of their absence of networks, politicking and cliques, mercenary cultures are usually meritocracies."[23]

This performance-based culture completely undermines the networked culture's system of building relationships to accomplish goals and secure positions within the organization. In an ideal mercenary culture, an individual who is not performing to an established ideal or is being difficult will be perceived as subverting the goal. Unlike someone in the networked culture, he or she will not be given the period of leniency or directed back into the collective fold. In an ideal mercenary culture, insufficient performance or failure is understood to be fatal to the individual's career, and little thought will be given to sparing the feelings of the difficult or nonproductive employee. As rough as this stance may sound, on a practical level it is often perceived by the other employees of a mercenary culture as a firm but just way of dealing with such issues.

Today's libraries face ever-changing organizational cultures. Whether a library tends toward a networked, mercenary, fragmented, or communal definition for its overall cultural orientation, different cultures can exist under one roof, each affecting the other, for better or worse. However, at any level of an organization, a managerial plan for working with change events, personal or group transition, and their resulting conflicts can only have a positive impact on the rest of the institution. Such a plan for change and conflict management must be considered an improved measure of the overall professional vision of any library professional for the organization.

TEAMS WITHIN AN ORGANIZATIONAL CULTURE

Alongside the four basic types of organizational cultures is the concept and idea of team management as an element within these cultures. Since the 1980s, a vacillating love-hate relationship has existed between the ideas of self-managed workplace teams and the various organizational structures and the managerial substructures contained within. Early case studies of team management in the professional business literature seemed to indicate that teams provided many positive effects to an organization. However, as the history or the idea developed, a gap seemed to occasionally appear, and "the connection between self-managed teams and effectiveness does not always exist in practice."[24] In many cases, upper management observed that teams often stagnated, became nonproductive, and even became a hindrance to the ideal for which they were formed. Such failures puzzled both management and researchers. The team concept was an idea that should work, yet aside from some success stories, why were there so many abject failures?

In one sense, a self-managed team is a organizational miniculture embedded in a larger one and hence reflects the larger organization's roles, relationships, policies, values, and communication styles while creating its own versions as well. Factors that impact this evolution of a miniculture include the gender, educational levels, cultural backgrounds, and current positions within the organizational group from which the members originated. This is especially true in teams that are organized from divergent groups within an organization.

The first question in deciding to implement a workplace team structure is whether or not the workplace or the organization really needs a team. As Richard Gallagher states, "A team building environment requires the right values. When management and employees don't trust each other, communication is poor, or workplaces suffer from departmental myopia, teams cannot happen no matter how much infrastructure you put behind them."[25] Also, the decision must carry more weight than simply following another organization's implementation of a team structure. A "monkey see, monkey do" approach can be a recipe for disaster. Any serious approach to team management planning requires an understanding of one's organizational culture and a serious analysis of one's own managerial motives and agendas. Questions to ask include

- Why do I, as a manager or administrator, want to bring team management into my organization? What issues or problems need resolution? Do I have a clear goal in mind for a team to accomplish?
- How does my organization organize authority and allocate power within the organization? Is the decision-making power centralized in a single individual (director) or a small group of people (department heads), or is it dispersed throughout the organization? Empowerment of and support afforded to teams is a critical factor to their success or failure.

Additionally, recent management study findings "suggest that teams with high levels of self-management may be more effective in organizations where the authority to make decisions about task performance is distributed, and in organizations with fewer explicit rules, policies and procedures."[26]

Is the organization going to be comfortable with sharing power with a team management structure if this has never been a part of its institutional history? It may not be pleasant to engage in this form of critical self-analysis, but it is absolutely essential to the process of organizing and implementing teams in the organization. What role does professional status play in your organization? Is there a hierarchy, pecking order, or class system? What values have you placed on professional academic credentials as conveying status and authority? Whether you personally or openly acknowledge a structure of this type, you can rest assured that the members of your organization are aware of its presence. Remember that in a typically fragmented academic culture, people derive their emotional and personal sustenance from their association with an academic discipline and may even view their role in the library as a necessity rather than a genuine calling. If such a culture exists, a cross-departmental, multilevel team may not be appropriate for your organization without significant modification of its organizational culture.

Do you really know or care how your managers and staff feel about their work environment? Do they know how you actually perceive the work environment and their roles within it? William Umiker asserts that "an organizational culture is the way things are done especially when no one is looking" and that many leaders "may fail to articulate the nature of their corporate culture or what they describe may be far from reality."[27] If the honest answer to these questions is a question in itself, a detailed analysis may be necessary before you proceed with team management.

How does your organization handle problems or resolve issues that arise in the workplace? Are managers expected to resolve their own problems, or is there a stated or unstated need to always seek input from a higher authority? How is a crisis handled? Does an atmosphere of crisis seem to always be present? You may find that you have what is termed a toxic organization or "one that thrives on control and exists in a constant state of crisis—depends on disasters and impending doom to make changes. Such change is often a short-term fix, rather than a well-thought-out solution to a problem."[28]

Do you, as an administrator, like to know what is happening in every part of the organization, or are you content to trust those under you to work out problems appropriate to their position? How were you personally taught to view authority, handle crisis, and make decisions? Were you given autonomy and responsibility, or were you required to seek permission and counsel before acting? As trivial as these questions may seem, an honest attempt to answer them may reveal whether or not you and your organization can handle the challenges presented by implementing management teams. In fact, the planning and implementing of teams may induce a major change in your organization. If at the end of this careful analysis, study, and soul-searching, your organizational culture is ill suited for the team concept, then the most responsible approach would be to simply forget the whole matter and continue as always. There is certainly no shame in admitting that your organization will not be better served by all the changes that real team management will induce or that your culture is simply not adapted to this innovation. Trying to force team management into the wrong culture will bring nothing but frustration, resistance, conflict, and overall disruption of what may be a functional environment. On the other hand, as Richard Gallagher reminds us, once you are implementing the team management concept into your culture, it must become culturally integrated; "To succeed in the long run, teamwork must go beyond a process or a program, to become an ingrained part of your culture."[29]

LEADERSHIP: THE FINAL INGREDIENT OF
ORGANIZATIONAL OR TEAM MANAGEMENT

Leadership is one of those terms that has been bandied around by librarians for decades without a clear, commonly accepted definition, any real understanding of why it matters, or how the concept of leadership might be applied to a library organization. The *Encyclopedia of Library History* states "the terms 'administration' and 'management' often have been used synonymously in the library field."[30] This misuse of terminology leads to a great deal of misidentification and confusion of roles and practices. The ability to "administrate" the policies and procedures of an organization is only a part of the overall package of managerial skills needed by today's librarian. Historically, as Charles Williamson stated, "no one specifically connected the philosophy of library services with efficient library management."[31]

However, since the 1980s, as libraries' budgets have grown and shrunk, costs for materials and resources have skyrocketed, and delivery of traditional as well as new proactive services has become the expectation rather than the exception. More libraries have come to adopt organizational postures similar to those of the commercial sector. In the world of professional librarianship, innovation and the changes that must come as a result of the above outside factors were not always welcomed in the library's organizational culture. Reactions to changes in the work environment often focused on maintaining the standards and status quo of previous generations. That adherence to tradition and precedent often treated creative thinkers with suspicion and thwarted their efforts or at least made any change an uphill struggle. In recent years technology has been the driving force in many library organizations; however, as Donald Riggs points out, "the mission of libraries has not changed due to technology, but the way the mission is achieved has changed dramatically."[32]

Out of these changes in expectations have come increased expectations of accountability, measurable results regarding services, and an ever-increasing expectation of productivity. With the proliferation of online resources, libraries have found themselves trying to justify their very existence in this new information age. The traditional passive "scholar in residence" approach to the profession and

its attendant "let them come to us" posture toward patron popula-
tions has become an unwelcome relic that actually works against the
continued vitality of the library. In order to survive and thrive in the
new information age, we must conceptually and organizationally
cease selecting our professional leadership strictly on the basis of academic credentials but on the basis of demonstrated managerial
ability. As two well-known library consultants indicate, "the hyper
speed of changes in information services now demands libraries that
are lean, mobile and strategic. They must be lean to meet expanding
customer expectations within the confines of limited budgets; mobile to move quickly and easily with technological and other innovations; and strategic to anticipate and plan for market changes."[33]

Managers are different in focus and function from leaders. As
Donald Riggs indicates, managers "tend to work within defined
bounds of known quantities, using well-established techniques to
accomplish predetermined ends, the manager tends to stress means
and neglect ends."[34] Managers deal with the organizational elements of the known, established work environment and are focused
on the process and procedures in those elements. Theirs is a structured and controlled perception of the world as it is and one given
to variation or innovation. Managerial skills and leadership are not,
however, mutually exclusive. Both have their distinct value to the
organization. In an ideal situation they would work together in a
balanced manner to produce optimal results.

Leadership, in American and European culture, has traditionally
had a mystique surrounding it and was often thought to have a di-
vine or quasi-magical origin. In reality, leadership has clearly been
demonstrated to be a learned and practiced skill. Leadership trainers swarm the world of business, offering, sometimes at considerable cost, seminars and sessions on acquiring this set of personal
skills.

What traits and characteristics constitute leadership as it differs
and relates to management? Consider the following commonly held
ideas concerning leadership:

Leaders are able to articulate and communicate their often original
   ideas and help others envision the possibilities contained in
   those ideas.
Leaders inspire, persuade, motivate, and challenge people to
   achieve and get results. They integrate themselves and their

ideas into the organization in a skillful and politically savvy manner.

Leaders are willing to take risks and can turn their and others' mistakes, conflicts, and failures into learning opportunities, and focus away from blame assignment.

Leaders know how to manage money and understand the language and concepts of their financial world. They are comfortable with ideas surrounding fiscal cycles, budgeting, allocations, and the reporting of financial matters.

Leaders know themselves as persons and managers; they use their strengths and acknowledge and work with their weaknesses. They self-evaluate and welcome the evaluations of others. They manage the world of perceptions and impressions around and about themselves.

Leaders are able to effectively affect change at the organizational level and lead their people through the transitional phases to adaptation.

Leaders embrace diversity and conceptually move beyond the barriers of gender, race, and social class in their recruiting, mentoring, and promotion policies.

Leaders realize the interconnected nature of events and relationships. They know their words, ideas, and actions have effects that move throughout their organization. Leaders take time to analyze those connections and their possible impacts before they speak or act officially.

Leaders help people educate themselves as to how to lead or manage themselves and others, often by modeling the kinds of behaviors that they wish others to develop.

Leaders share their power as a way to increase their power and influence. If information is power, then sharing that information is more powerful.

Leaders have a vision of what is realistically possible and manage that vision in a practical, achievable manner. They also know how to sell that vision to others. As a result, there is a strong element of salesmanship and perhaps evangelization in the qualities of leadership. For librarianship leadership means being able to convey the enthusiasm and dedication for the service internal to the profession. Leadership creates and fosters an atmosphere of pride and excellence in service that no seminar or single presentation can transmit.

Leaders in librarianship, like leaders everywhere, fully understand the dynamics of the organizational environment and can operate successfully at the organizational, cognitive, and emotional levels. They are realistic visionaries who understand how to secure and evolve the organizational culture as they bring about different changes. They view actions with a systemic view and continually assess the progress of their ideas, altering them as needed to achieve the long-range goal, whether that goal is team management or any other.

NOTES

1. William Taylor, "Organizational Cultures and Administrative Leadership in Universities," in Thomas J. Sergiovanni and John E. Corbally, eds., *Leadership and Organizational Culture: New Perspectives on Administrative Theory and Practice* (Chicago: University of Illinois Press, 1984), 125–41, 131.

2. William Umiker, "Organizational Culture: The Role of Management and Supervisors," *Health Care Manager* 17, no. 4 (June 1999): 23.

3. William Sannwald, "Understanding Organizational Culture," *Library Administration and Management* 14, no. 1 (Winter 2000): 8.

4. Sannwald, "Understanding Organizational Culture," 8.

5. Sannwald, "Understanding Organizational Culture," 9.

6. Sannwald, "Understanding Organizational Culture," 9.

7. Sannwald, "Understanding Organizational Culture," 12.

8. Jasmine Tata and Sameer Prasad, "Team Self-Management, Organizational Structure, and Judgments of Team Effectiveness," *Journal of Managerial Issues* 16, no. 2 (Summer 2004): 249.

9. Rob Goffee and Gareth Jones, *The Character of a Corporation: How Your Company's Culture Can Make or Break Your Business* (New York: Harper Business, 1998), xiv.

10. Taylor, "Culture and Leadership in Universities," 129–130.

11. Goffee and Jones, *The Character of a Corporation*, 147.

12. Goffee and Jones, *The Character of a Corporation*, 163.

13. Goffee and Jones, *The Character of a Corporation*, 123.

14. Goffee and Jones, *The Character of a Corporation*, 124.

15. Goffee and Jones, *The Character of a Corporation*, 128.

16. Jack G. Montgomery and Eleanor I. Cook, *Managing Conflict in Library Organizations: Strategies for a Positive, Productive Workplace* (Chicago: American Library Association, 2005).

17. Goffee and Jones, *The Character of a Corporation*, 128.

18. Goffee and Jones, *The Character of a Corporation*, 131.

19. Goffee and Jones, *The Character of a Corporation*, 73.

20. Goffee and Jones, *The Character of a Corporation*, 81.

21. Riane Eisler, "From Domination to Partnership: The Hidden Subtext of Organization Change," *Training and Development* 49, no. 2 (February 1995): 7.

22. Goffee and Jones, *The Character of a Corporation*, 99.

23. Goffee and Jones, *The Character of a Corporation*, 108.

24. Tata and Prasad, "Team Self-Management," 248.

25. Richard S. Gallagher, *The Soul of an Organization: Understanding the Values That Drive Successful Corporate Cultures* (Chicago: Dearborn Trade Publishing, 2003), 95.

26. Tata and Prasad, "Team Self-Management," 257.

27. Umiker, "Organizational Culture," 22.

28. Cynthia Coccia, "Avoiding a 'Toxic' Organization," *Nursing Management* 29, no. 5 (May 1998): 32.

29. Gallagher, *The Soul of an Organization*, 95.

30. Jane Rosenberg, "Library Management," in Wayne A.Wiegand and Donald G. Davis, eds., *Encyclopedia of Library History* (New York: Garland, 1994), 373.

31. Jane Rosenberg, "Library Management," in Wayne A.Wiegand and Donald G. Davis, eds., *Encyclopedia of Library History* (New York: Garland, 1994), 374.

32. Donald Riggs, "The Crisis and Opportunities in Library Leadership," *Journal of Library Administration* 32, nos. 3/4 (2001): 9.

33. Becky Schreiber and John Shannon, "Developing Library Leaders for the 21st Century," *Journal of Library Administration* 32, nos. 3/4 (2001): 36.

34. Riggs, "The Crisis and Opportunities in Library Leadership," 6.

Chapter 2

When Is a Team Really a Team? Examples of Team-Based Management Concepts in Academic Libraries

Michael Norman

For many years, academic libraries have searched for effective management structures to make their technical services departments (TSD) as productive as possible. In the 1990s, several large academic libraries introduced teams and team concepts into their acquisitions and cataloging units with the goal of improving production and the work environment of employees. This chapter analyzes the introduction of team structures in the libraries of five universities: the University of Arizona, the University of New Mexico, Pennsylvania State University, the University of Kentucky, and the University of California, Irvine. An examination shows there were many similarities and common occurrences in the reorganizations of these libraries. At about the same time, the University of Illinois, Urbana-Champaign, (UIUC) Library introduced teams and team concepts into its TSD, and this study looks at this implementation and how it has impacted the current organizational structure. As technical services departments migrate from the print to the digital world, the use of teams could help libraries retool their organizations.

Libraries exist in a complicated world. At the University of Illinois, Urbana-Champaign (UIUC) Library, users have come to expect comprehensive access to digital and electronic collections twenty-four hours a day and seven days a week, from their homes, offices, dorm rooms, and even local coffee shops and Internet cafes. Academic libraries of all sizes and shapes have had to figure out how to provide access to full-text resources, link resolution, and federated searching, and how to deal with digital library initiatives, educational portals, repositories (institutional, national, and international in scope), cataloging and harvesting of digital objects and metadata, and archiving and preservation of digital information. How do libraries, and the technical services departments serving them, provide the most efficient access to these new initiatives and resources? How does a library's technical services department re-create itself to continue acquiring, cataloging, and processing the traditional library materials (books, serials, CD-ROMS, microforms, audiovisual materials, etc.) while at the same time meeting the added demands of dealing with digital resources? Librarians have been asking these questions for the past ten to fifteen years. As Karen Calhoun at Cornell University Library expertly puts it, "It is a defining moment for technical services departments, which are being asked to do more work with the same or fewer resources at a time when they must find ways to become involved in new library initiatives."[1]

In the mid-1990s, to help deal with the added demands of the beginning stages of many of these new initiatives, and also due to decreasing budgets and increasing prices for all purchases, many academic libraries, including the UIUC Library, introduced team-based management structures and concepts into their technical services departments to become more efficient and cost effective. Team structures had been used successfully in the business world, and many academic libraries began to synthesize the team management concepts to fit into a library setting and incorporate them into their technical services departments to deal with the high volumes of acquiring, cataloging, and processing of materials. These reorganizations were initial steps taken to restructure faculty and support staff into viable and effective organizational configurations that established both the flexibility and adaptability needed to deal with the electronic and digital resources increasingly sought by their user communities.

There were many benefits to utilizing the team structure in academic libraries. By involving all employees in planning, functionality, and communication, teams allowed greater use of the talents and abilities of all their employees. Respect and trust for others was a central concept. More people, including all levels of staff, were involved with decision making, which usually occurred through consensus. Open communication and collaboration became essential. Cross-functionality became a reality that created the ability to move quickly and adapt to changing organizational (and library) needs. Most importantly, the team structure produced self-sufficient and self-directed units that could be directed to deal with new or old challenges. Over the course of the implementations, many of the same team concepts emerged at many academic libraries. Many of these characteristics have become important components to running a successful library in the twenty-first century, especially as libraries try to become more agile in dealing with the challenges of the future. Many of the team concepts revealed in this study are present in the technical services units at the UIUC Library. The word "team" is not used as frequently as it once was. But many team concepts are in existence today and play an important role in creating an environment that allows faculty and support staff to deal successfully with providing access to information for the library's user community.

This chapter examines the implementation of team-based organization in the technical services departments in the libraries of five universities: the University of Arizona, the University of New Mexico, Pennsylvania State University, the University of Kentucky, and the University of California, Irvine. Their reorganizations are analyzed and a list of team concepts is produced to look at the comparable experiences and occurrences at these academic libraries. Second, this study examines the implementation of team-based technical services management at the UIUC Library and, finally, the evolution of team-based organization at UIUC a decade later is explored.

TEAM MANAGEMENT STRUCTURE IN LIBRARIES

The concept of team management has been around for many years, originating in the late 1960s. But in the early 1980s, influential individuals in the business and management worlds such as Peter Block, Charles Aubrey, Patricia K. Felkins, W. Edwards Deming, Tom Peters, Rosabeth Kanter, and Peter Drucker[2] put forth the team-based structure as the best way to get the most out of "all" the people working for a business or organization. As teams and team management became more popular in the 1990s, authors such as W. Glenn Parker, Fran Rees, Dave Francis, and Don Young published works that looked at improving team concepts and allowing organizations and their workers to get the most out of the team-based experience, including ways to make meetings more productive, train better team leaders, involve everyone in planning, introduce evaluative tools to measure productivity, and maximize the input of every employee.[3] Always at the heart of these publications was the importance of the organization's employees. As Calhoun notes regarding libraries, "People are the key to success, together with what they know, their attitudes and behaviors, how they choose to do their work, the tasks they are assigned, and the processes they use."[4] The examination of team management implementations in this chapter shows that people and their willingness to participate in the new structures played an important part in the success of the implementation.

A search of the literature shows that several libraries became interested in the team concept in the mid-1980s and into the early 1990s, hoping to mimic the successes occurring in the business world. The list of libraries implementing some form of team management structure is long and includes Texas Tech University Libraries, Pennsylvania State University Libraries, University of Kentucky Libraries, University of New Mexico General Library, Indiana University–Purdue University, Indianapolis, Library, Southern Mississippi University Library, SUNY College of Fredonia's Reed Library, University of California, Irvine, Libraries, and the University of Arizona Library, among others. Libraries were beginning to feel the impact of many concurrent factors, including shrinking budgets, rising costs, and the advent of new formats and resource types. Automation and integrated systems brought different ways to order, acquire, catalog, and process these disparate resources. The organizational structures in place in many libraries were no longer sufficient to handle the changing nature of daily functions and user services. Having to do more work with fewer resources and individuals, some libraries began to turn to team management to utilize the full potential of their workforces and make their work as effective and productive as possible.

UNIVERSITY OF ARIZONA LIBRARY

One of the first academic libraries to implement teams and team management into their organizational structure was the University of Arizona Library. With the hiring of Carla Stoffle as library director in 1991, the library began a study to determine the best organizational structure to save costs and improve services in a time of fiscal challenge with continually decreasing budgets. Over the span of eighteen months, which included bringing in consultants from the Association of Research Libraries, the library chose a team-based management structure as the best fit and, in 1993, set out to reorganize the entire library into a new organizational structure. All areas, including technical services, were reorganized into teams.

As Diaz and Pintozzi write in their article about the organizational restructuring, there were several guiding principles involved with the reorganization, including a focus on customers/users, empowerment of individuals and teams to make decisions for which they have appropriate information, knowledge, and skill base, creating the proper functionality through training for all employees, establishing effective communication lines, forming an evaluative assessment approach to ensure that services to users were efficient and effective, and incorporating an impetus toward change to ensure that the teams and the library continued to look toward the future with decision making.[5] Carrie Russell wrote in another article assessing the move to teams at the University of Arizona Library, "The current organization is based on the premise that the collaborative team environment inspires staff motivation and innovation as they work on ways to better serve the user by solving problems, improving processes, planning for the future, implementing strategies, and committing to continuous learning and organizational development to benefit the user."[6]

The library reported many positive changes and a few challenges resulting from the reorganization. A flexible team-based structure had been created. Staff members were "relatively happy with where they are and . . . are developing skills needed to do their jobs effectively."[7] The position of assistant dean for team facilitation was created, and the dean helped the various teams define goals, made sure everyone participated in the functioning of the teams, resolved problems and conflicts, and reinforced goal setting as a priority. Some of the negatives and challenges resulting from the reorganization included the realization that continued staff training was a must, communication between individuals and teams was extremely important, implementing evaluation of team performance did not come easily, and introducing a way to reward and compensate staff for good work was unresolved. Overall, in 1999, when the

University of Arizona Library reassessed the move to team-based management, they defined the reorganization into teams as "remaining dynamic, flexible, and implementing ongoing change."[8] They reiterated that "the people of the organization and their commitment to providing quality services to their customers are the engine that will continue to propel the library into the future."[9] According to the authors, teams and team concepts were key components for the University of Arizona Library to provide valued library service to its users.

UNIVERSITY OF NEW MEXICO GENERAL LIBRARY

The University of Arizona Library was one of the first academic libraries to implement team-based management into its overall organizational structure and also its technical services department, but several other prominent academic libraries were also trying out team structures. David Baldwin, then dean of library services at the University of New Mexico, writes that he and his colleagues at the University of New Mexico General Library (UNMGL) wanted an organizational system that provided the best possible service for the state's flagship institution of higher learning. As Baldwin and Robert Migneault document in their book, *Humanistic Management by Teamwork: An Organizational and Administrative Alternative for Academic Libraries*, UNMGL implemented a team management approach called Humanistic Management by Teamwork (HMBT) to bring about "an effective and efficient management system . . . [while] the UNMGL faculty and staff have had the remarkable ability to advance the university libraries in the face of ever-increasing demands and expectations and limited resources."[10]

Humanistic Management by Teamwork (HMBT), as advocated by Migneault, concentrated on teamwork and putting its employees at the center of the organizational mission. This included making sure no employee was underestimated, realizing employees represent the gamut of individually possessed values, capacities, and traits, that all expressed ideas of employees are potentially useful, and that the collective yield of all employees was greater than that produced by a few.[11] At UNMGL, teams would become responsible for establishing programs, determining priorities, assigning responsibilities, and allocating monies.

UNMGL had several goals in mind when they implemented the team management concept, including creating principles of respect for each other; more participation in decision making; producing greater flexibility and adaptability among its workers and organizations; using work groups, task forces, and project teams within this new structure to get work done faster; and creating opportunities for teams and work groups to have members from the different departments across the library interact.[12] They agreed with Calhoun's assessment of the importance of people in the new structure. The authors put an emphasis on how "[team] members must be motivated to work with others; they must bring their knowledge to the team; they must collectively have the needed authority to make decisions; and the team membership must be changed as the situation or goal of the team changes."[13] Baldwin and Migneault came to realize that the critical part of the success of introducing team-based management is that each member of the team and the overall organization share the same values and goals in order to move the library forward to become more efficient, effective, and productive. High morale, self-esteem, and pride in the organization were desired results for all employees of the library. In 1996, the authors declared the move to HMBT and team-based management, for both the overall library and its technical services department, a success and advocated the move for other libraries.

PENNSYLVANIA STATE UNIVERSITY LIBRARIES

One of the most extensive studies done on the implementation of a team-based structure in technical services occurred at the Pennsylvania State University (PSU) Libraries through their adoption of Continuous Quality Improvement (CQI), a version of Total Quality Management (TQM), in the early 1990s. Nancy Markle Stanley and Rosann Bazirjian, through a series of articles, describe the reorganization of the technical services department over the span of seven years at the PSU Libraries. In the third article in the series, Bazirjian and Stanley look at the results of an assessment done on the new organizational structure that was introduced in 1994 for the Acquisitions and Cataloging departments. Separate surveys were developed, one for technical services and one for public services, to evaluate the effectiveness of the team structures in technical services. This publication is one of the few examples of a library reporting their findings through a survey of the individuals involved in the team management structure.

It was anticipated at PSU Libraries that reorganization into teams would produce "improved communications and enhanced customer service,"[14] matching the same expectations of the University of Arizona Library and the University of New Mexico General Library. There was also a desire to improve staff morale through training, empowerment, and better communication. Self-directed work teams (SDWT) were created to make a group of workers "responsible for a whole work process,"[15] including setting goals and priorities, training fellow team members, evaluating productivity of the team and individual members, and selecting a team leader of the month to coordinate the actions of the group. These self-directed teams were introduced in the mid-1990s and continued to function at the time of the survey and article in 2001.

From the results of the survey, the PSU Libraries discerned that most employees in technical services preferred the self-directed team approach over the organizational structures of the past. The survey listed positives within the comment sections, but the survey also revealed areas that needed improvement within the team structure, including finding ways to handle poor performance, disciplinary actions, and instituting a rewards and recognition program for good work. Encouragingly, the survey also revealed that the majority of individuals felt that teams should continue to be responsible for monitoring the completion of work, for training others, for determining the priority of work, for decision making related to tasks, for defining the performance standards of the group, and for delegating responsibility to team members for completion of the work.[16]

The authors concluded that "self-directed teams work best in areas where supervision only gets in the way and where creativity rather than process and procedure are the norm."[17] One of the important aspects that becomes clear from their study is that it requires many years, usually a span of two to five years, to advance to "fully empowered teams."[18]

UNIVERSITY OF KENTUCKY LIBRARIES

Almost at the same time as PSU Libraries' switch to self-directed teams, the University of Kentucky Libraries initiated a redesign and reorganization of the technical services departments to position it-self for a projected move into a new library. The director of libraries stated that "he did not wish to take a 1950s organization into a state-of-the-art facility designed to serve the University in the 21st cen-tury."[19] In 1996, the Monograph Processing Team was set up. It had many goals, including (1) providing access to information resources in all formats as quickly and effectively as possible; (2) developing and maintaining a simple seamless processing flow, which is effi-cient, effective, and prevents backlogs; (3) ensuring high-quality products and services; (4) developing and maintaining a customer-oriented focus for technical processing; and (5) establishing and supporting a work atmosphere that offers staff training and staff op-portunities to the fullest extent.[20] As with several of the other li-braries involved in this study, most of the staff were new to the team environment. The library introduced them to the important concepts of team management through multiple information sessions that in-cluded looking at vision, goals, empowerment, decision by consen-sus, group dynamics, and productivity standards. In 1998, when the University of Kentucky opened its new library, as Mary McLaren re-ports in her article, a process-based model was adopted for the Monograph Processing Team, and this produced a new model that achieved "more staff cross-training, flexibility, fewer hand-offs of materials to other persons, more efficient searching and processing procedures, the incorporation of gifts and shelf preparation proce-dures, . . . the incorporation of some cataloging with the acquisitions receipt process, and the implementation of outsourced cataloging services."[21] By the time the library moved, the technical services de-partment at the University of Kentucky Libraries had successfully adopted the team structure and gained greater flexibility and effi-ciency to deal with the ever-changing world of electronic and digi-tal resources.

UNIVERSITY OF CALIFORNIA, IRVINE, LIBRARIES

In 1997, the libraries at the University of California, Irvine (UCI), an-nounced that "the UCI Libraries have become a learning organiza-tion with a firmly established team culture."[22] Although they had used the word "team" often to describe other organizational struc-tures used in the past, including many temporary and short-term groups, most staff at the UCI Libraries did not have a true under-standing of the meaning of team management. As Joanne R. Euster, Judith Paquette, Judy Kaufman, and George Soete state in their 1997 article, it took many months to get everyone up to speed and de-velop the "teamliness" desired to make the changes to implement this new organizational structure.[23] Four teams were created, includ-ing Collections and Access Services, Personnel and Administration, Research and Instructional Services, and Technical Services. As with many other libraries, these teams formed around functional respon-sibility but also had authority across physical boundaries.

Almost all the staff at UCI Libraries participated by attending meetings, workshops, and training sessions to prepare them for the new structure that incorporated stable membership in functional/operational teams and a way to provide short-term teams to deal with projects or sudden problems. When the staff were asked if they would like to go back to the old organization, Soete notes that they began to cite the positive results over the negative. One interesting note the authors brought out was that "some sug-gested that they felt they had a real say in the decision-making process for the first time."[24] The administration at UCI Libraries declared that the introduction of team-based management was a success and echoed many of the other libraries in this study who claimed greater flexibility and better responsiveness to the changes occurring around them.

COMMON ASPECTS OF TEAM MANAGEMENT IN LIBRARIES

Several common aspects and concepts emerge from the libraries that were able to successfully integrate teams into the organizational structure of the libraries and their technical services departments. These concepts include the following:

- In most libraries, team management is a radical culture change, and it might take years to get it right.
- Many of the teams and groupings created at these libraries in-cluded librarians and staff both within and outside each func-tional group.
- All members of the libraries are involved and participate by at-tending frequent meetings, presentations, training sessions,

and seminars on team building, team dynamics, conflict resolution, and team leadership skills.

- Decisions made by the team need to involve everyone and are made by consensus.
- A strong team leader is needed to keep the group directed and involved.
- It is important to have productivity measures in place to ensure that the work is being done efficiently and in a timely manner.
- The ultimate result of team-based management is to provide better services to the library's user community, an overarching library value.
- Active and constant communication with everyone involved in the reorganization is one of the key ingredients to a successful reorganization.
- Outside consultants (frequently from the Association of Research Libraries) are essential to help evaluate, review, redesign, and help guide the organization through the process.
- Teams should form around recognized needs of the library.
- Libraries will gain greater flexibility and adaptability throughout the reorganization to deal with day-to-day workflows and the introduction of new projects and tasks.
- For most libraries, a full understanding of the implications of how teams might function did not occur until after the reorganization and individual interaction in a group had occurred.

As demonstrated by the experiences of these libraries, these concepts and ideals are ones that most libraries wanted to possess in dealing with, and providing service to, the informational world that was developing. Each sought the involvement of all employees, decisions made by consensus, open communication, the ability of individuals to have cross-functionality to be able to do work across the technical services spectrum, and the flexible, adaptable, and agile team-based structures to afford library administration and staff methods by which to deal with new situations when they are encountered.

INTRODUCTION OF TEAMS IN
TECHNICAL SERVICES AT UIUC LIBRARY

An examination of these five academic libraries shows they encountered many of the same situations and circumstances in reorganizing into team-based management structures and experienced many of the same positive and negative results. Not every encounter was the same, but most of the libraries reported the introduction of teams as a successful endeavor in preparing them for the future. In 1998, the Technical Services Division at UIUC Library (UIUC TSD) also took the plunge and moved away from its unit-based organizational structure and reorganized into four process-related teams: Original Cataloging, Rapid Cataloging, Serials Cataloging, and Acquisitions. It had been nearly ten years since the library had completed a decentralization of original cataloging by moving those functions out to the departmental libraries while centralizing most of the processing functions such as OCLC Copy Cataloging, OCLC Support Services, Automated Records Maintenance, Serials Cataloging, Office of the Principal Cataloger, and Auxiliary Cataloging Services (which was responsible for providing cataloging support and training) into an Automated Services Department.[25] The Acquisitions Department had remained outside the organizational umbrella of the Automated Services Department but was incorporated into the larger Technical Services Division.

There were several coalescing factors that led to the restructuring of UIUC TSD in 1998, including (1) the implementation of the library's first integrated library system, the DRA Classic system; (2) the need to regroup faculty and staff into an organizational structure that moved away from compartmentalized and separate functions into an environment that produced more flexibility and cross-functionality to acquire, catalog, and process materials; and (3) the upgrading of the skills and abilities of all TSD employees to deal with the technologies needed to automate many cataloging and acquisitions processes, including Microsoft Windows, an integrated library system, OCLC services, and so on. The reorganization to team-based management for UIUC TSD was deemed the best way to deal with these factors and move the library forward to providing more efficient service to the library's user community.

INTRODUCTION OF THE DRA CLASSIC SYSTEM

An important factor in this whole reorganization was the UIUC Library's plans to migrate in 1998 from its homegrown Library Computer System (LCS) to the integrated DRA Classic system. The

LCS was developed by UIUC in 1978 and served as the library's circulation system. It was populated with short non-MARC bibliographic records that consisted of call number, author, title, edition, place of publication, date of publication, Library of Congress card number, and holdings information. LCS could not take full advantage of the MARC bibliographic records being created within OCLC. The library turned to the Western Library Network (WLN) for a way to incorporate full MARC records and augment the capabilities of the LCS circulation system. Through the purchase of the WLN system, which the UIUC Library called Full Bibliographic Record (FBR), and a customized linking method, the LCS system became the circulation system, while FBR enabled the library to use MARC records for the first time. The library had to maintain its acquisition, business, and check-in information in separate systems or paper files. For the UIUC Library, LCS, FBR, a homegrown acquisitions system to record acquisition and business information, serial check-in cards, and other individual systems supplied the overall mechanism for providing library services for almost twenty years, from 1978 to 1998. Daily functions and workflows within the TSD units required utilization of all of these systems to process materials. Moving to an integrated system would require everyone to learn new technologies, skills, procedures, processes, and workflows.

Between 1995 and 1998, the UIUC Library, along with the Illinois Library Computer Systems Organization (ILCSO) state-wide consortium, moved to implement the DRA Classic system. According to Bregman and Burger, "The choice of DRA was based on its promise to create an integrated system different from any that existed. This system was called Taos."[26] To implement DRA, the UIUC Library created implementation teams for acquisitions, serials control, cataloging, public access to the online system, circulation, and technical transition. This was the first time a team-based structure had been utilized at the library. Training workshops were conducted to familiarize team members with the dynamics of working in teams, interacting with others, utilizing conflict management, ground rules for meetings, and other important components of successfully utilizing teams and team concepts.

Unfortunately, the selection of DRA Classic never satisfied the library's desire to have an integrated library system (ILS). Over the course of migrating to the DRA system, portions of the system were never implemented, including the acquisitions and serials control modules. Taos never became the functioning online integrated system the library or the ILCSO consortium wanted. The library and ILCSO would have to wait another four years to have a fully functioning ILS, when they implemented Endeavor's Voyager system in 2002–2003. Many of the plans set in motion for the DRA Classic implementation and an integrated working environment would have to be put on hold.

TEAM STRUCTURE IN UIUC TSD

Even with the limitations of DRA Classic, the restructuring and re-naming of the technical service units proceeded. Recommendations included the following:

- The Division of Technical Services should be organized along team lines, taking into account the workflow processes that currently cut across Acquisitions, Automated Services (Cataloging), and the Office of the Principal Cataloger.
- A new Acquisitions Team should be established within Technical Services to carry out acquisitions (vendor selection, ordering, claiming, approving payments, and receipt of library materials).
- A new Serials Cataloging Team should be formed within Technical Services, made up of all staff in Automated Services and the Office of the Principal Cataloger currently involved with searching, cataloging, and final processing of serials.
- A new Rapid Cataloging Team should be formed within Technical Services to be made up of current OCLC Cataloging, including searching and inputting staff involved with processing monographs as copy.
- A new Original Cataloging Team should be formed within Technical Services to be made up of the current Auxiliary Cataloging faculty, one member of the Office of the Principal Cataloger, and members of Support Services.
- Team leaders should attend courses in management, staff supervision, and team leadership. Team leaders and team members should participate in orientation sessions familiarizing them with the concept of team organization.

- The coordinator of Technical Services should be charged with ensuring the development and coordinating the activities of efficiently working teams in the reorganized division.[27]

Many of these recommendations mirror what happened at the five academic libraries analyzed in the first part of this chapter. The teams at UIUC TSD were to be centered on processing and recurring activities. Each team would have a leader to help direct the team's actions, and an overall coordinator of Technical Services would ensure collaboration and successful interaction between the four teams. Cross-functionality and flexibility to deal with integrated workflows was a desired outcome. Finally, it was suggested that team leaders and team members attend and participate in sessions to help familiarize themselves with working in a team structure.

In the fall of 1998, these recommendations were instituted by the UIUC Library. Four librarians (who would become the leaders of their respective teams) and fifty-six support staff were reorganized into the four process-based teams including Acquisitions, Serials Cataloging, Original Cataloging, and Rapid Cataloging. The overall division was given the following charge:

> Each Technical Services Team shall be responsible for coordinating all activities respective to their individual areas of technical services processing. This will include (but may not be limited to) setting policies and standards for the team's tasks, revising and reengineering workflows as appropriate to provide the most accurate and efficient processing possible, identifying and pursuing new technologies and procedures which will expedite and enhance the team's tasks, and providing adequate and effective communication lines to other teams within Technical Services and also other library units.
>
> Upon formation, each team will be required to establish a written set of goals and objectives which must include a complete Customer Service plan. This plan must contain the following: 1) Communication Policy for a system for communicating with other teams, system for communicating with other library units, and system of documenting and communicating workflow and procedural changes; 2) System of Benchmarking which includes defining and communicating meaningful statistics, defining the objective quality of job performance, and personal performance benchmarking; and, 3) Ground rules for internal team behavior and procedures.[28]

Each individual TSD team had a separate charge. For example, the Serials Cataloging Team's charge was to accurately represent serials and their holdings in the library online catalog, to continue to deal with the check-in of serials, continuations, and analytics received directly in Acquisitions, to move materials through the system in a timely manner, and to maintain accurate holdings records within the catalog.

Teams were given ground rules (with lists distributed to team members to have at their desks) to help facilitate the creation of a true team environment. The rules included these:

- At every meeting, everyone has the chance to talk.
- Every member will receive respect and appreciation for what he or she brings to the team.
- Each member of the team has value and merit and has the right to voice an opinion.
- Every member is responsible for providing an opinion.
- We will discuss a decision until we have a solution that everyone can live with.
- We will revisit issues/procedures—procedures need to stay fluid to change with new information.
- We need to understand all pieces of the process.
- We will offer feedback in a positive way.
- We will share our knowledge with everyone on the team and communicate it to other teams in writing and e-mail.
- Agendas will be open and will be circulated in advance of meetings; decisions made at meetings will be recorded and distributed.

All of these actions were a promising start for the TSD division. There were several reports in the *Library Office Notes* (*LON*), the UIUC Library's internal newsletter, describing how the reengineering of TSD had fared.[29] Similar to the other libraries in this study, there was also a little anxiety with the changes being instituted, particularly with how particular individuals would fit into the overall workflow of getting materials out to the users.

One of the major hurdles to solidifying the team structures in TSD at this time was the failure of the DRA Classic system to become a true integrated system. Work would have to continue in separate systems for the foreseeable future. As Bregman and Burger state,

"UIUC Library's bold move to put faith in a promising but barely developed system was based on the vision of truly integrated library processes. . . . It was assumed that the integrated system would be the catalyst to institution-wide change."[30] This change would have to wait, however, as the planned system was never realized.

Over the following years, many of the aspects and concepts of teams and team management were not entirely realized. Initial training sessions, courses, workshops, and developmental opportunities to promote strong leadership skills, how teams worked, team dynamics, making meetings productive, and time management were held but never really moved beyond the beginning stages of development. For some teams, participation by all was not a reality. Many team members did not fully participate in the decisions being made by the team. Silence was a common occurrence at meetings, and communication was still a problem. Because of the lack of an integrated system, many workflows, procedures, and processes that would have required consultation, collaboration, trust building, and helping others get the work done and achieve success did not happen. However, this did not mean that the values of teams were not recognized. The concept of teams had been planted and would continue to grow over the next few years.

TEAM CONCEPTS AT UIUC TSD IN 2005

As mentioned earlier, the UIUC Library would have to wait another four years to have a fully functioning integrated library system (ILS). In July 2002, UIUC Library went live with Endeavor's Voyager system. It would take several years to fully implement the system. One of the tangibles of implementing Voyager over the past three years has been that "teamliness" has started to prevail in the day-to-day work that occurs within TSD. Workflows in both cataloging and acquisitions now intersect on a daily basis. The division has been able to gain full benefit from such features as approval plans, using PromptCat to automatically get bibliographic records of monographs ordered from vendors, outsourcing of materials to be cataloged, authority control, working to provide complete access to all the library's electronic and digital resources, incorporating vendor records into the online catalog, integrating link resolution and federated searching into the work done by TSD and others, and cross-training of staff in both Acquisitions and Monographic Cataloging to do the whole process of receiving and cataloging of materials.

The implementation of Voyager has played a role in this transformation. But over the past three to four years, there has been another important factor. Karen Calhoun's adage about the importance of people in the role of success has inserted itself into the daily work of the division. As she writes, "people are the key to success."[31] When DRA was implemented in 1998 and the team management structure implemented, the division had only four librarians to run the entire organization. TSD has many more librarians now, having added many new people to the faculty within the division, including six in cataloging, two in acquisitions, two in conservation and preservation, and several academic professionals rounding out the group. Adding these new people along with the innovation and energy of a new coordinator for Technical Services has brought about a willingness to work together to make the division as efficient and productive as possible. While there are still three unit heads within TSD and one division coordinator, the running of the various departments is presently shared, and everyone is encouraged to participate. Decisions are made by consensus. Information sessions regarding the work of all the departments are abundant in number, for both TSD and the library as a whole. Communication is much better. There is vibrancy and liveliness within the division, and teamwork and collaboration play a big part in getting much of the work done.

The division will be reorganizing once again over the next few years. Much of the work within TSD is still tied to the traditional print materials the library receives each day. But with more and more of the library's collection budget (estimated at 30 percent of the overall budget of $15 million for 2004–2005) going to electronic and digital resources, additional people, time, and effort will be needed to acquire and catalog these resources. Metadata creation is another activity that will need to be folded into the daily workflows of the librarians and staff within the division. Work on an institutional repository will begin later this year, as well as implementing a link resolver and federated search system. UIUC TSD will play an essential role in the success of these endeavors. To do all of this well will require the input of many people and not just one or two individuals. Team-based management with its inclusive and participatory nature by both librarians and support staff will be an integral component of effectively planning how the division is reorganized. Working as teams, with different individuals taking the role as leader, to deal with the many different developments and projects the library encounters will be an important aspect of the division successfully providing excellent service to the library and its user community.

CONCLUSION

Since the 1990s, teams and team concepts have played a major role in the organizational structures for some academic libraries and the technical services departments that serve them. With all the additional work and initiatives that technical service units have absorbed with the proliferation of the digital library in recent years, teams and the importance they put on the involvement of each individual within the organization to delivering the best possible service and access have become even more vital to libraries in meeting their users' needs.

This analysis of five academic libraries that implemented team-based management structures during the 1990s shows that these libraries did see some benefits from introducing teams into their TSD organizational structures. New contributions from employees were common, and more people were involved in decision making. Communication improved within technical services and throughout the library as collaboration and cross-functionality were regular occurrences. Self-directed teams could tackle new problems and challenges as they arose. Negatives did happen, such as spending much more time in meetings, responsibility for productivity was often left to the individual, evaluative measures and reward systems were hard to develop, and not everyone had the skills to be a strong leader.

At about the same time as the other five academic libraries were introducing teams into their TSD structures, UIUC TSD also reorganized along the team-based management structure. Teams and team concepts were identified as the best way to deal with the introduction of new technologies and improve productivity of all technical services functions to help deal with the growing informational needs of the library's user community. For several reasons, UIUC TSD did not have the same immediate success with restructuring the division into teams as the other five academic libraries encountered. However, many of the team concepts that emerged at these other libraries did eventually materialize at the UIUC Library as well. Individuals in UIUC TSD did grasp the importance of team concepts and pulled together to emphasize the important roles communication, collaboration, trust, and teamwork play in the success of an organization. The UIUC Library needed this implementation to occur also because many of these team concepts are integral to successfully dealing with the research needs of the library's users.

The word "team" is not prominent within the names of the different units within UIUC TSD anymore, but the all-important concepts and characteristics of teams are present within the people in the division and mirror many of the occurrences and successes of the other five academic libraries in this study.

NOTES

1. Karen Calhoun, "Technology, Productivity and Change in Library Technical Services," *Library Collections, Acquisitions, and Technical Services* 27, no. 3 (2003): 283.

2. There were several publications that came out in the 1980s that promoted team-based management. These include Peter Block, *The Empowered Manager: Positive Political Skills at Work* (San Francisco: Jossey-Bass, 1987); Charles A. Aubrey and Patricia K. Felkins, *Teamwork: Involving People in Quality and Productivity Improvement* (Milwaukee: Quality Press and American Society for Quality Control, 1985); W. Edwards Deming, *Quality, Productivity, and Competitive Position* (Cambridge: Massachusetts Institute of Technology, 1982); Thomas Peters, *Thriving on Chaos: Handbook for a Management Revolution* (New York: Knopf, 1987); Rosabeth Moss Kanter, *The Change Masters: Innovations for Productivity in the American Corporation* (New York: Simon & Schuster, 1983); Peter Drucker, "The New Society of Organizations," *Harvard Business Review* 70, no. 5 (1992): 95–105.

3. Several prominent publications came out in the 1990s expanding on the theories of teamwork in the 1980s. They included Glenn W. Parker, *Cross-functional Teams: Working with Allies, Enemies, and Other Strangers* (San Francisco: Jossey-Bass, 1994); Fran Rees, *How to Lead Work Teams: Facilitation Skills* (San Diego: Pfeiffer & Co., 1991); Dave Francis and Don Young, *Improving Work Groups: A Practical Manual for Team Building* (San Diego: Pfeiffer & Co., 1994).

4. Calhoun, "Technology, Productivity and Change," 288.

5. Joseph R. Diaz and Chestalene Pintozzi, "Helping Teams Work: Lessons Learned from the University of Arizona Library Reorganization," *Library Administration and Management* 13, no. 1 (1999): 32.

6. Carrie Russell, "Using Performance Measurement to Evaluate Teams and Organizational Effectiveness," *Library Administration & Management* 12, no. 3: 159.

7. Diaz and Pintozzi, "Helping Teams Work," 33.

8. Diaz and Pintozzi, "Helping Teams Work," 35.

9. Diaz and Pintozzi, "Helping Teams Work," 36.

10. David A. Baldwin and Robert LaLiberte Migneault, *Humanistic Management by Teamwork: An Organizational and Administrative Alternative for Academic Libraries* (Englewood, CO: Libraries Unlimited, Inc., 1996), 168.

11. Baldwin and Migneault, *Humanistic Management by Teamwork*, 166.

12. Baldwin and Migneault, *Humanistic Management by Teamwork*, 41.

13. Baldwin and Migneault, *Humanistic Management by Teamwork*, 73.

14. Rosann Bazirjian and Nancy Markle Stanley, "Assessing the Effectiveness of Team-Based Structures in Libraries," *Library Collections, Acquisitions, & Technical Services* 25 (2001): 138.

15. Bazirjian and Stanley, "Assessing the Effectiveness of Team-Based Structures," 132.

16. Bazirjian and Stanley, "Assessing the Effectiveness of Team-Based Structures," 138.

17. Bazirjian and Stanley, "Assessing the Effectiveness of Team-Based Structures," 142.

18. Bazirjian and Stanley, "Assessing the Effectiveness of Team-Based Structures," 137.

19. Mary McLaren, "Team Structure: Establishment and Evolution within Technical Services at the University of Kentucky Libraries," *Library Collections, Acquisitions, and Technical Services* 25 (2001): 358.

20. McLaren, "Team Structure," 360.

21. McLaren, "Team Structure," 364.

22. Joanne Euster, Judith Paquette, Judy Kaufman, and George Soete, "Reorganizing for a Changing Information World," *Library Administration and Management* 11, no. 2 (1997): 104.

23. Euster et al., "Reorganizing for a Changing Information World," 111.

24. Euster et al., "Reorganizing for a Changing Information World," 113.

25. Michael Gorman, "Reorganization at the University of Illinois—Urbana/Champaign Library: A Case Study," *Journal of Academic Librarianship* (September 1983): 224.

26. Alvan Bregman and Robert H. Burger, "Library Automation at the University of Illinois at Urbana-Champaign, 1965–2000: A Case Study of Technological and Organizational Validity," *IEEE Annals of the History of Computing* 24, no. 2 (2002): 81.

27. Alvan Bregman, *First Report on Reengineering Technical Services: Reorganization of Automated Services and the Office of the Principal Cataloger, University of Illinois Library, Urbana-Champaign* (Urbana: University of Illinois at Urbana-Champaign Library, 1998).

28. UIUC Library, *Technical Services Team Charge* (Urbana: University of Illinois at Urbana-Champaign Library, 1998).

29. UIUC Library, "Executive Committee Minutes," *Library Office Notes* 25 (July 1998).

30. Bregman and Burger, "Library Automation at the University of Illinois at Urbana-Champaign," 84.

31. Calhoun, "Technology, Productivity and Change," 288.

Chapter 3

Teams and the Control of Work: A Case Study at Arizona

Michael S. Ray

Librarians and support staff in a team-based organization contend with the disruption of their tasks brought on by innovations in information technology. Team approaches to organization promise each member greater flexibility and opportunity to learn, but if these opportunities are to be realized, the employees must be willing to find and secure jurisdiction over new tasks. Given their position in the hierarchy of control over tasks, this ability to change tasks is different for librarians compared to the support staff with whom they work. The team organization does not guarantee equality of opportunity in the face of other occupational groups competing for the same task jurisdictions in an economically stressed university setting. This chapter updates and extends a 1997–1999 study of jurisdictional shifts in library work responsibilities at the University of Arizona (UA) and explores the consequent changes in the team structure and job duties of library specialists occupied with technical work once provided solely by librarians. The following questions direct the inquiry upon which this chapter is based:

1. *How have library specialists been ceded tasks by librarians in both the acquisition and circulation sides of technical services?*
2. *What is the relationship of librarians (and their professional project) to other occupational groups in the emerging technical environment?*
3. *How does team organization handle the emerging changes?*

The original research was based on in-depth interviews over a broad sample of team members, conducted by the author. This chapter updates that

original research with findings from a variety of continuing research efforts
conducted as part of the author's involvement as an employee at the library,
as well as an internal consultant and team member in a human resources
position.

The chapter concludes with a look forward at the continuing transfor-
mation of technology in technical library work, the role of team structure in
adapting to these changes, and potential impacts on professional and tech-
nical positions in the team.

TEAMS AND SOCIOTECHNICAL SYSTEMS

"If a technical system is created at the expense of a social system, the
results obtained will be sub-optimal."[1]

This quote summarizes an important principle of sociotechnical
design as practiced by the Tavistock Institute of Human Relations in
London. Eric Trist, a founding member of the institute, studied un-
employment that resulted when the jute industry introduced new
technologies in the late 1930s. He saw the introduction causing
deskilling and alienation, and concluded that the technical and social systems were in conflict. The insights from Tavistock, along with
the pioneering work of Kurt Lewin (survey research) and Douglas
McGregor (laboratory training), provided substance for the human
relations movement, which ultimately gave encouragement to a
multitude of professional projects such as organizational development, total quality management, and informatics. Social psychology
and the study of group dynamics combined to change our concep-
tion of employee motivation and involvement. As a result, small
groups, and then teams, became the centerpiece of a participatory
approach to creation and production in business.

Today, a similar threat of deskilling and alienation accompanies
the introduction of new forms of information access in the modern
library. The advent of outsourcing of cataloging to OCLC and other
vendors assisted copy cataloging in the past decade (this started in
the early 1990s), and the recent rapid growth in use of Google and
other search engines to find books and journal articles without the
mediation of a library catalog illustrates the challenges to library
tasks and competencies.

Technology and team-based forms of organization provide customer value in a new global economy. All are drivers for change in

occupational work. Segments of the U.S. economy, particularly manufacturing, were among the first to adopt team approaches to production in the 1980s when foreign manufacturers in major sectors such as automobiles began the massive restructuring of manufacturing power away from the United States. Increased use of teams took root when it became obvious that a structural over-reliance on management-centered decision making was incapable of addressing the cost, speed, and quality required in a global marketplace.

Education and professional organizations experienced some built-in buffers against these market forces and a natural reluctance to take the team approach as a central organizing principle. State-supported higher education guaranteed faculty with tenure a place to teach and research for life. But in the last decade the restructuring of many states' budgets is bringing a set of constraints and imperatives for change much like those in the private sector to bear on public-sector jobs. The professional model of faculty control over work is challenged by new economic and technological imperatives:

- Blended approaches to learning that combine classroom learning with virtual and action learning resources in the field
- Interdisciplinary approaches to complex research questions that shift the practice to collaborative, rather than singular, approaches to knowledge production

In status hierarchies the more highly ranked professional decision makers rule their domains. In an academic environment, librarians serve the interests of ranked faculty and seek a similar status. Masters-level certification does not provide the certification and expertise in research needed for librarians to attain complete parity with faculty, so their centrality to the scholarly process is not a given. The historic dimensions of the librarian's jurisdiction in the scholarly communication process are undergoing transformation. Cataloging has been automated and outsourced. Reference questions are mediated by search engines. Selection lists are brokered with vendors. When technology intervenes, altering the central role of librarians in the access of information for scholarly communication, librarians find themselves contending with graduate students, computing, and student services professionals for tasks in the emerging teaching and research environment.

Teams struggle to form or operate in status hierarchies. Faculty ranks and the academic department represent the interests of professionals seeking to maintain control over their own work. The agility and customer focus sought by administrators needing to diversify sources of revenue and cut costs are often achieved only by restructuring the organization into groups or teams that cut across old dominions, and then at a high political cost. Team forms of organization face barriers to the incorporation of members from multiple stakeholders, occupational levels, or groups. In many places the only team you see operating is what would otherwise be called a task force or problem-solving group with a tightly focused purpose and limited authority.

SHIFTING SANDS AT THE UNIVERSITY OF ARIZONA

The University of Arizona Main Library system was among the first to comprehensively adopt a team structure and consequent reliance on employees at every level for decision making, transforming a professional hierarchy in the process. This is a story covered in depth in other works.[2-7]

In the shift to teams, the UA Library recognized that it needed a new social system to match up with an emerging technical system based not on shelves and card catalogs but on electronic access to information through the Internet. By the mid-1990s it became clear that the progeny of this decision would be the digital library. In making the strategic argument for employee involvement, the shift to teams cultivated the seedbed for changes in the very nature of work itself, including the shift of job duties from one occupational group to another. This was not an explicit part of the vision, but an inherent value in seeing the organization as a more open system, one in which the importance of self-managing groups and the need to address problems of workplace alienation would force upon librarians a set of demands that could not be ignored.

The social system is complex. It is also political. All parties are not equally provided with decision-making power. Teams perform to the expectations of an administered organization. The administered organization responds to its economic, technical, and cultural environment with a variety of strategies, including changes in allocation and sources of funding (retrenchment), recruitment and hiring, layoffs, reorganization, outsourcing, training, process improvement, and strategic partnerships with other organizations. Change reflected in these strategies may occur centrally or emerge at any time from the periphery of the organization as new players in economic markets emerge.

The initial case study research was conducted at the University of Arizona Main Library over a three-year period from 1997 to 1999. The qualitative method employed in the study sought to answer the following questions:

1. As information services and the management of knowledge grow in economic importance, how do ongoing changes in information delivery, copyright/fair use, and intellectual property engage academic librarians and put pressure on their choice of activities?

2. How do librarians actively strategize and assert themselves in contending with other occupational groups (faculty, publishers) for (or with indifference to) jurisdiction over information technology–enabled services and products?

These questions and the answers gained from the case study research provided the basis for development of a "grounded theory" in which the categories and dimensions of the data gathered provided the core understanding of problems and processes driving changes in the jurisdiction of tasks. Observations and activities are labeled and grouped into concepts. Concepts are developed into categories with properties and dimensions that can be linked, resulting in the discovery and specification of differences among and within categories, as well as similarities.[8] Only after the patterns discovered in the data have themselves spoken are they compared to extant theories of occupational control over tasks.[9, 10]

IMPACT OF TEAMS ON PROFESSIONAL TASKS

For the purposes of this chapter, two dimensions from the study tell us much about the impact of teams on technical service jobs: *status* and *competencies in use* (see Figure 3.1). The dimension of *status* here includes notions of both professional privilege and decision-making power, and the perceived value or importance of tasks assigned to

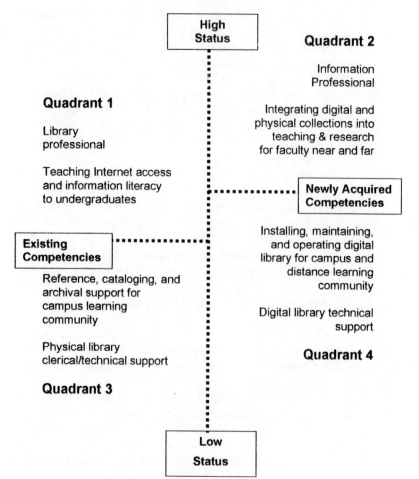

Figure 3.1. The Grounded Theory's Two Primary Dimensions: Competencies with Status

professionals, high or low. The *competencies* dimension is temporal, referring to both those competencies with current or historic relevance and those that are emergent, uncertain, or newly acquired.

Together, these two dimensions are related as the demand for new competencies has shifted the value of historic library tasks, organized as it has been around selection and access to materials. There is a shift in task jurisdictions among the professional library workforce from those historic tasks associated with the library professional to a new set of tasks associated with what some would call the information management professional. This same shift can be seen with the paraprofessional library support staff as they move from library clerical and technical support in a world of physical objects to digital library technical support in a virtual world from which the routine clerical tasks are removed through automation or outsourcing.

Among the extant theories applied to the patterns that appeared in the data on jurisdictions are those of Andrew Abbott. Abbott theorizes that professions exist by right of control over techniques and abstract knowledge, influenced by differentiation in clients, intellectual jurisdictions, and settlements reached through the division of labor. Abbott sees key events as those that create or destroy jurisdictions. Because no profession is an island, their interactions must be viewed as a system, in which professional struggle occurs at three levels: the institutional setting, culture and public opinion, and legal and administrative policy. Finally, Abbott articulates a theory that successful professions maintain a monopoly over a core jurisdiction, which may grow and change as the profession delegates off old knowledge and seeks dominance over new knowledge.

> Each profession is bound to a set of tasks by ties of jurisdiction, the strengths and weaknesses of these ties being established in the processes of actual professional work. Since none of these links is absolute or permanent, the professions make up an interacting system, an ecology. Professions compete within this system, and a profession's success reflects as much the situations of its competitors and the system structure as it does the profession's own efforts.[11]

Abbott's analysis falls short in two aspects important to this case study: (1) His analytical framework does not explicitly recognize the system of professions as existing within a larger system of capitalism, in which profit and nonprofit organizations vie for jurisdiction over markets for information products and services, and (2) he says very little about the control exercised over professional groups in large organizations by institutional decision makers, assuming for the most part that jurisdictional strategies are made by professionals for their peers, in competition with the claims made by surrounding competitors to librarianship—"the audiovisual people, the artificial intelligence people, the computer people."[12] Abbott glosses the critical impact of administrators and professional managers who, at least in large organizations, deploy the many professional skilled employees of the organization, and whose interests may not coincide completely with the professionals they oversee.[13]

At the library in the case study, the limitation in Abbott's theory is particularly important, because a significant number of professionals and support staff together forged an agreement to change the organization in 1993 and put in place principles that would turn professionals into process managers and make the organization less focused on professional prestige and more focused on cost and customer requirements. This involved a significant shift away from a hierarchical decision-making authority vested in senior librarians toward a distributed decision-making model based on shared leadership.

While not studied in depth here, this shift happened with the blessing of the president and the provost of the university. In all matters financial and relative to university policy, their support is crucial. With their support, the degree of freedom from human resource and other policies that would have stood in the way of team relationships was overcome. The administrative regime changed from a traditional dean/director and four associate university librarians making most key decisions to one in which decision making was distributed among five major stakeholders:

- The dean (with a focus on external relations and the faculty)
- The library cabinet (consisting of the dean, functional team leaders, and representatives of governance groups—focused on internal policy and support of teams)
- The functional teams, facilitated by a team leader, who are collectively responsible for establishing a yearly operational plan, quality standards for work, and performance plans for each team member with developmental goals that are peer reviewed three times a year
- An Information Resources Council (staffed by librarians representing the selectors who spend the information resources budget, responsible to allocate that budget)
- The Strategic Long-Range Planning team is staffed by both librarians and support staff with multiyear terms of office, who develop the five-year strategic plan, and are joined by the dean to determine the budget for the plan. This team is responsible for conducting a current situation analysis each year, reviewing

mission and vision, and developing a focus on the vital few improvements or actions needed each year to pursue the objectives of the plan. The resulting areas of focus are vetted with the functional teams and cabinet and often result in the formation of strategic cross-functionally staffed project teams.

As this "shared-governance" approach took shape, "it was clear that all the embedded systems that had supported work in the former organizational structure were incompatible with the new structure and goals. Every system—from the leadership and hiring systems to work process design and performance management—would have to change."[14] The historic control over tasks exercised by senior librarians, from this point on, would have to contend with a hydra-headed administrative system that was not amenable to elite professional control. That control would now be subject to review and public reasoning by an increasingly federated and complex assortment of occupational groups organized in a variety of functional and cross-functional teams. Increasingly, the definition of professional work would also face scrutiny.

In the beginning, the first challenge to professional tasks came from the realization that the library could not expect university administrators to fund a comprehensive print collection. "In 1989 the University of Arizona Library administrators charged a task force . . . to investigate the impact of rising serials prices on the library's ability to continue to build high-quality research collections. . . . [This] led the task force to recommend that the library pursue an 'access' strategy in the future in order to ensure its success."[15] This initial change in direction diminished the centrality of bibliographic selection prowess among the librarians.

When, in 1991, the new dean formed a steering committee to complete a self-study, deciding how the organization should be structured, this committee decided the library should become a team-based, customer-focused, quality learning organization. Those employed at the library who experienced a professional identity forged in areas of expertise such as selection, cataloging, and reference often enough viewed the customer as needy and themselves as the required resource. Years of professional experience were equated with a higher level of competence in providing standards of professional service. By the early 1990s three factors were about to rend the historic value of professional expertise in selection, cataloging, and reference: service costs, flexible organization structures (including teams), and information technology innovation.

At the UA Library, administrative power in the organization today is distributed among the dean, the library cabinet, functional teams, and numerous cross-functional teams. Additionally these groups operate in the context of a shared governance framework that consists of a Library Faculty Assembly (LFA) and a Staff Governance Association (SGA). Centrally planned project teams managed and charged by these administrative groups are often the agents of institutional-level change, utilizing process improvement concepts incorporating planning, analysis, and implementation in their relatively brief lifetimes. Functional teams are also a source of planning, some of which is more emergent as positions turn over, or unforeseen events unfold. The support they receive for making changes in the jurisdiction of tasks (who will do what in a crisis or new service delivery situation?) comes from human resource and financial systems, as well as informally from colleagues.

In the team-based technical services environment of the UA Library in 2005, the work of many functional and cross-functional project teams, charged and managed by administrative groups, is reshaping the ground on which team members stand. Financial reports are updated each month so that each team knows where it stands. Some teams have been converted from state funding to revenue-funded units with business plans. Human resource and organizational effectiveness support takes the form of team building and process improvement facilitation and expertise from internal and (occasionally) external consultants.

This reshaping began with the reorganization from a hierarchical to a team-based organization in 1993. Since then several generations of process improvement, outsourcing, and reorganization have continued to change the way work is accomplished. Here is a brief synopsis of the kinds of changes observed:

- In 1993 the technical and access services were organized into two teams. Librarians accompanied support staff into these teams, but the largest concentrations of professional positions were organized into "Integrated Services" teams devoted to providing instruction and selection services to specific academic sectors: science and engineering, fine arts and humanities, social sciences, undergraduate studies, and special collections.

- In 1997 the acquisition services outsourced some cataloging to OCLC and demarcated what remained of the cataloging librarian's tasks to library specialists. This shifted the jurisdiction of what were core librarian tasks to occupational groups that do not require a Master of Library Science degree. The cataloging librarians moved to the Integrated Services teams where they were expected to become selectors and instructors.
- In 1997 a functional team developed a project group to tackle issues of digitization of special collections. By 1999 that group became a functional team dedicated to producing digital products, producing new titles for librarians such as copyright librarian and metadata librarian. In 2002 that group was combined with the library's Information Technology Support group under a single team leader.
- In 2002 a new information commons facility connected to and managed by the library opened to wide acclaim. The 300 computers loaded with the latest software required extensive training of the supporting staff.
- By 2002 the changes noted above resulted in a strategic project team forming to analyze the staffing of functional teams, and recommended the reformation or combining of several teams. The Fine Arts Team and Special Collections (both supporting branch operations) were combined under a single team leader.
- In 2005 a strategic project team researched and reshaped the staffing model for the entirety of the reference services in the system, directly impacting both branch and main service sites, and the many teams that staff those sites. Questions logged at the many sites revealed the inefficiency of staffing those sites with librarians who committed only six hours a week to a site that provided directional and general reference responses 95 percent of the time. Circulation and reference desks were combined, and trained paraprofessionals in technical services took on sole responsibility for the service at branch sites. In the heavily used information commons, librarians on a team now work ten hours a week each, provide both walk-up and virtual chat services, and are responsible for managing the entire reference system.
- In 2005, a study of the library's access and delivery mission was in process, and librarians were looking at the need to radically revise their educational and collection development assumptions.

- In human resources, a study of the changing job duties of library specialists, the most often used support staff title at the library, was underway to consider the need for a new level of description for the competencies required and a new title and classification for the work being done.

Cross-functional project teams with administrative power to reshape fundamental dimensions of service provide the institutional response to rapidly changing social and technical trends in the use of library resources. As a byproduct of these projects, the task dimensions of librarians and support staff are also shifted, and what was once the exclusive jurisdiction of librarians over tasks is demarcated to subordinate groups or outsourced. Among librarians and support staff this progression of events is generating anxiety, excitement, and a dialogue about the future of their occupational work.

SHIFTING SANDS—RECENT EVENTS

Since the completion of the "Shifting Sands" study in 1999, the status and competencies dimensions generated by the original research can be more clearly seen. The cataloging duties that were outsourced have created a vacancy in knowledge about metadata cataloging at the same time that questions about knowledge management for support of faculty instruction and research continue to grow.[16] The continued withdrawal of state support for budgets has caused the library to look at the cost of reference and instruction services. For the first time, librarians are applying process improvement methods to their core work, and both reference and instruction services are the target. The resulting logic of cost containment in a cultural and technological context of search engines seeks to repurpose librarians from traditional librarian tasks to information management roles.

In both the material acquisition and circulation realms the competencies needed to perform the work are changing, and both professional and paraprofessional support staff are impacted.

The value of digital library concepts such as metadata, rights management, and archiving may rest in the hands of administrators and diverse faculty interested primarily in their own bottom line: What is the return on investment for the primary research of time spent managing these issues?[17] Yet the competency required to answer simple directional or basic reference questions (95 percent of all transactions as logged recently at the Information Commons) is a far cry from the competency required to broker the use of digital tools and archiving services in the remade digital library of the future.

Mastery-level competencies in collection development, information resource development, education, and reference services are being recast,[18] often requiring quite different skills and knowledge than were taught in library school or supported by professional societies. The technical services needed to support the new services while simultaneously maintaining legacy print collections likewise undergo change. In a team-based technical services environment, the empowerment and self-direction of classified staff is propelling them toward job duties that quickly outdate job descriptions and market comparisons.

Reorganization within and among teams is a primary method used by administrators to address the loss of positions, need for reskilling, and development of new service roles for the employee workforce. Through attrition rather than layoff, the UA Library technical staff lost forty or more positions over ten years. At the same time the remaining staff became more efficient and skilled through process improvement studies and organization reviews that led to raising the standards of performance and competency required for their changed job duties.

The HR compensation system was reformed to support these shifts. A pay-for-skill program called Career Progression was put in place in 1997. Salaries among library specialists in technical services were largely in the lowest quartile of the range. Today those salaries are largely at or above the midpoint of the range.[19]

The need for competitive pay and flexibility in assignments that accompanied working in teams led the UA Library to cease using its entry-level "library assistant" and "library assistant senior" positions. Instead, an ad hoc broadband was adopted in which we now hire only "library specialists." Reclassification of our existing library assistants and assistant seniors was predicated on their ability to demonstrate the skills and knowledge needed to perform at that level. Career Progression pay is used to raise salaries as incumbent capabilities increase within the current position.

Accompanying this shift in responsibilities and skills is the need to change the market comparisons. Whenever market adjustment funds are made available for classified staff positions, comparisons are made with other local institutions (city/county library and community college library). A study of the comparison positions in these other contexts finds them completely out of alignment with the nature of the work responsibilities now performed by library specialists in the UA Library. This established the need for a change in title and description.

In realms such as managing suppliers, cross-functional teaming, budgeting, and performance appraisal, team-based technical service members develop capabilities that blur the lines between the team leader and the team members.[20]

At the UA Library the study of library specialists, who are the primary workforce in technical services, illustrates this blurring effect. As many as one-quarter of the staff with the library specialist title direct other staff, sometimes in a permanent lead position, sometimes as part of a rotation on and off a decision-making team, or as a temporary assignment to special duty. Supervisory positions still exist but are greatly reduced in comparison to the preteam structure. These "specialists" are in fact becoming "generalists" as they develop through cross-functional assignments a broader understanding of technical services and the larger library operations. They take on the more complex assignments. They provide coaching but don't initiate disciplinary reviews. That is ceded to supervisory titles. The generalists join developmental reviews of specialists. They assist in site management. They take leadership of project teams and demonstrate facilitation skills. Taken together, their generalist competency makes them indispensable to management in a team-based environment where supervisory title and control have become less valuable than facilitating the rapid expansion of knowledge and overall understanding of operations in a rapidly changing technical environment.

THE PROMISE OF TEAMS—FOUNDATION
FOR LARGER COLLABORATIVE EFFORTS

Librarians face a challenging search for new tasks to replace those that have been lost or given away. Their own functional team environment is not sufficient to provide the opportunities and openings into these new tasks. What is needed is a collaborative framework with faculty, graduate teaching assistants, and suppliers of information "solutions." They need to create and seize opportunities to build the collaborative instructional and research "teams" that are increasingly relevant to work in a "blended" teaching environment and interdisciplinary research. Their relationship to faculty projects in these arenas is crucial to demonstrating the value of their knowledge. Their new roles will likely evolve more toward consulting and brokering of information systems and involve less standing behind a reference desk or instructing an undergraduate class, though these roles may continue in a more limited way.

In the technical services team, where librarians' numbers are much fewer, their embrace of technical knowledge and ability to broker the emerging technical system will be a key. Support staff in these areas take on the tasks delegated to them from the librarians and increase their value as paraprofessionals with higher salaries and titles. Routine clerical work is systematically outsourced and automated. The technical systems they maintain are increasingly complex and mediated by vendors. They must monitor these systems and collaborate with technicians to maintain functionality lest the systems fail to provide service.

Librarians and support staff are supported by the team form of organization to the extent that the team leadership and dialogue provide for the direction needed, the training and development to support the direction, and the ability to put the right people together to rapidly address a problem or opportunity. As they demonstrate these capabilities, members of teams perform with a flexibility and speed never demonstrated under more hierarchical and status-dominated forms of organization.

NOTES

1. Enid Mumford, *Socio-Technical Design.* www.enid.u-net.com/Sociotech .htm (accessed January 18, 2005).

2. Laura J. Bender, "Team Organization—Learning Organization: The University of Arizona Four Years into It," *Information Outlook: The Monthly Magazine of the Special Libraries Association* 1, no. 9 (1997): 19–22.

3. Joseph Diaz and Shelley Phipps, "The Evolution of the Roles of Staff and Team Development in a Changing Organization: The University of Arizona Library Experience," in *Finding Common Ground: Creating the Library of the Future without Diminishing the Library of the Past,* ed. Cheryl LaGuardia and Barbara Mitchell (New York: Neal-Schuman, 1998), 408–23.

4. Joseph Diaz and Chestalene Pintozzi, "Helping Teams Work: Lessons Learned from the University of Arizona Library Reorganization," *Library Administration and Management* 13, no. 1 (1999): 27–36.

5. Shelley E. Phipps, "Performance Measurement as a Methodology for Assessing Team and Individual Performance: The University of Arizona Library Experience," *Proceedings of the Third Northumbria International Conference on Performance Measurement in Libraries and Information Services* (August 27–31, 1999): 113–117. Newcastle-upon-Tyne, England: Information North for the School of Information Studies, University of Northumbria at Newcastle. Available online at www.library.arizona.edu/library/teams/fast/biblio.html.

6. Shelley E. Phipps, "The System Design Approach to Organizational Development: The University of Arizona Model," *Library Trends* 53, no. 1 (2004): 68–111.

7. Carla Stoffle and Shelley Phipps, "Meaningful Measures for Libraries," *Library Issues* 23, no. 4 (2003): 1–4.

8. Anselm Strauss and Juliet Corbin, *Basics of Qualitative Research: Grounded Theory Procedures and Techniques* (Newbury Park, CA: Sage, 1990).

9. Andrew Abbott, *The System of Professions* (Chicago: The University of Chicago Press, 1988).

10. Andrea Witz, *Professions and Patriarchy* (New York: Routledge, 1990).

11. Abbott, *The System of Professions*, 33.

12. Abbott, *The System of Professions*, 439.

13. Gary Rhoades, *Managed Professionals* (Albany: State University of New York Press, 1998).

14. Phipps, "The System Design Approach," 72.

15. Phipps, "The System Design Approach," 70.

16. Sara M. Pritchard, Smiti Anand, and Larry Carver, "Informatics and Knowledge Management for Faculty Research Data," *Educause Center for Applied Research (ECAR) Bulletin*, no. 2 (January 18, 2005): 1–14.

17. Pritchard, Anand, and Carver, "Informatics and Knowledge Management," 7.

18. Karen Holloway, "Developing Core and Mastery-Level Competencies for Librarians," *Library Administration and Management* 17, no. 2 (Spring 2003): 94–98.

19. Michael Ray, "Rewarding Strategic Learning and Performance: The Experience at the University of Arizona," *Library Administration and Management* 18, no. 3 (Summer, 2004): 8–17.

20. Rosann Bazirjian and Nancy M. Stanley, "Assessing the Effectiveness of Team-Based Structures in Libraries," *Library Collections, Acquisition, & Technical Services* 25, no. 2, (2001): 131–157.

Part 2

EFFECTIVENESS OF THE TEAM STRUCTURE

Chapter 4

University of Maryland Libraries: Case Study for Program Review

M. Sue Baughman, Gordana Ruth, and Janet L. Siar

Changing technology, an aging workforce, and shrinking budgets are forces that drive libraries to carefully examine their existing structures and services. The major restructuring of an organization is a complex effort that takes a large amount of time and energy and requires institutional support. Program review is a valuable tool that an organization can use to envision its future. Critical components of a program review include creating a vision, collecting and analyzing data, recommending changes, implementing practical strategies, and evaluating the outcome. This chapter describes the steps the University of Maryland Libraries' Technical Services Division took in the process of organizational change from a hierarchical structure to a team-based structure.

The University of Maryland (UM) Libraries' Technical Services Division (TSD) conducted a program review in 2000–2001. The purpose of this review was to assess current workflow patterns, identify new work patterns for increased efficiencies, and revise the organizational and staffing structures to better accommodate the revised workflows. This program review and implementation process engaged every member of the Technical Services staff and took a little over a year to accomplish.

The newly proposed organizational structure resulted in the formation of both production groups that focus on the day-to-day operations and coordinating teams that focus on workflows among various groups and teams. This chapter presents an overview of the program review process and discusses the importance of assessing the development of teams within the organization, especially in reviewing workflows. It also describes the rationale for moving to team-based Technical Services, the value of networking teams within a larger organization, and the successes and challenges of a wide-scale change process in a division of over sixty librarians and staff.

TEAMS IN THE UM LIBRARIES

Technical Services program review and subsequent team development occurred within a broader context of team development across the UM Libraries. During the 1997–1998 academic year, the University of Maryland Libraries began a process of assessing current services provided to faculty and students. The impetus behind this evolution of change focused on several key issues. First, a new director of public services joined the libraries in 1997, providing an opportunity for new leadership and a review of the Public Services Division's operations. Second, some members of the organization perceived that there was a duplication of effort and expertise under the current organizational structure in the manner in which librarians in two different divisions, the Public Services Division and Collection Management and Special Collections Division, worked with the teaching faculty. There was also an issue of inconsistent service to academic units on campus. Such factors resulted in library administration appointing a Services Task Force, which was charged with addressing the need for improved services in the main library, McKeldin, and the six branches. The work of this task force resulted in a new service model for McKeldin Library as well as the articulation of a philosophy of service for all of the UM Libraries.

Implementation of this new service model and philosophy took shape with the formation of three disciplinary subject teams in the summer of 1998: social sciences and allied professions, science and technology, and humanities and fine arts. Librarians previously assigned to two separate divisions were brought together around the various disciplines to provide reference, instruction, and collection management services. Team leaders were appointed to lead the work of these teams.

This was a major change for the libraries, which formerly operated as a more traditional, hierarchical organization with department heads and unit supervisors who behaved in a directive manner. These new teams were asked not only to rethink how service was being provided to faculty and students, but also to change some of their own behaviors regarding management styles, decision-making processes, and how job responsibilities were carried out.

In 2000, the dean of libraries, Charles Lowry, wrote the libraries' first working paper, "Team Management: The Vision of a Team-Based Learning Organization,"[1] which described several principles for the continued development of the organization. These principles were the following:

- The libraries will provide quality products and services of high value to customers (students, faculty, and administration).
- Teamwork and partnerships will be the way work is accomplished with a specific focus on teams becoming self-managing.
- Effective practices will be identified and consistently incorporated into work processes.
- The libraries will study, measure, and analyze the structure of work and focus on the ongoing improvement of work processes and systems.
- As a learning organization, continuous education and training are paramount in the pursuit of individual and organizational excellence.
- Change will be continuous as the libraries and teams discover the best way to work and the right work to do.

Since 2000 further developments have included the formation of other teams, creation of new programs to support the organization, and other significant changes for the libraries. Functional program teams, with membership of both librarians and staff from the libraries' five divisions, were formed in 2000 to address policies and procedures related to reference and information services, information literacy, collection management, and access services (circulation, reserves, and interlibrary loan). These teams are known as the Information and Research Services Team, Information Literacy Team, Collection Management Team, and Access Services Team, respectively. Each of these teams has a leader, whose primary responsibility is the area of the program. Members apply for team membership and serve terms of two to three years.

Another major organizational change for the libraries occurred in 2000 when librarians obtained non–tenure track faculty status. Library faculty and staff developed a faculty Plan of Governance as well as a promotion and permanent status process. Librarians now document their yearly progress and development in three areas: librarianship, service and scholarship, and creativity.

A comprehensive learning and education program, the Learning Curriculum, was initiated in 2001. This program focuses on skill development in areas such as customer service, teamwork, leadership, measurement and assessment, meeting effectiveness, time management, stress management, and computer skills. The Libraries' Office for Staff Learning and Development manages this program by evaluating training needs and developing and carrying out programs.

The Facilitators Team, a library-wide team of six members, was organized in 2001 with the purpose of facilitating organizational change and improvement through the use of a variety of group process activities and tools. Facilitators work with groups, committees, other teams, and task forces on short- or long-term assignments; facilitate one-time events; and conduct training on the use of group process tools.

In 2003, the Leaders Group formed as a way to improve and strengthen communication across the libraries. Members of this group include team leaders for subject, program, and production group, and branch teams. Other members are those individuals with responsibility for programmatic areas such as management information systems, human resources, development, and so on.

Most recently, the Collection Management and Special Collections Division began a review of the special collections departments in 2004 to develop new vision and mission statements and to determine the most effective organizational structure. The Special Collections Working Group recommended that several subject and functional teams be established. For example, one subject team will be the Historic Preservation Team, and a functional team will be the Orientation and Training Team. As a result, teams continue to evolve and grow within and throughout the organization.

TECHNICAL SERVICES PROGRAM REVIEW

Technical Services program review began soon after Carlen Ruschoff joined the libraries as the new TSD director in March 2000. At a meeting in April with all TSD staff, she noted that a number of significant changes were occurring within the division and the libraries that would strongly affect the work of technical services. The most important of these were the retirements and turnover of people in positions in key areas, a shift in library goals and objectives to increased focus on faculty and students, continuous change due to evolving technology, and the switch from a text-based integrated library system (ILS) to a Windows-based ILS. These changes provided an opportunity to review and evaluate current activities and operations within the division. The new director worked with outside consultants, the current TSD deputy director, and department heads to design a suitable framework for this review process. She maintained close communication with the dean of libraries and the other divisional directors throughout the process.

The program review was initiated in the summer of 2000. The first step in the process was to examine the current structure of the division, paying particular attention to workflows, bottlenecks, and other problems. There were several overarching goals for this review:

1. All staff in Technical Services as well as staff from other divisions would be engaged in various steps in the process.
2. The process guiding the work would include gathering data, identifying benchmarks, getting input from internal customers, drafting a proposal, and gathering feedback on the proposed recommendations.
3. Deliberations and recommendations would incorporate the libraries' vision of a team-based learning organization.
4. Recommendations would be reflective of thinking in new ways about how the work of technical services needs to be done in order to support the research mission of the university and the mission of the libraries.

The TSD director met with all TSD staff in June 2000 to discuss the goals, methodology, and timetable for the program review. Based upon the major processes currently taking place within the division, eleven working groups were formed. Each group developed a thorough analysis of its processes and procedures. This assessment was accomplished by creating macro- and microflowcharts and detailed descriptions of various tasks. One working group focused on gaining information about organizational structures for technical services from the University of Maryland's institutional peers. The groups concluded their work by submitting written reports, as well as presentations in group discussions, that not only highlighted the flow of work, but also served to identify bottlenecks, other concerns, and ideas for possible improvements.

BLUE RIBBON COMMITTEE (BRC)

As the working groups were completing their charge, staff throughout the libraries were invited to apply for membership to a Blue Ribbon Committee, to be tasked with recommending a new organizational structure. The director of TSD served as the chair of this committee, and a facilitator from the Facilitators Team supported the work of this group. The BRC began its work in December 2000, with the following charge:

> To recommend an overall organizational design for Technical Services that (1) streamlines functions and eliminates duplication of effort, (2) insures cost-effectiveness, (3) is flexible and evolves with changes in division goals, new technologies, and enhanced procedures, (4) incorporates the principles of teams, (5) expresses an integrated relationship with the overall library organization. The Committee is further charged with recommending changes in practice and procedures to eliminate redundancy as well as identify areas that require a process improvement study or new work initiatives. In conducting its work, the Committee will rely upon the following background documents: the Division's Mission Statement, the Libraries' Strategic Plan, the Libraries' Working Papers, the Program Review Reports, the Program Review "key messages," articles from the library literature on reorganization as well as core values which will be articulated by the Committee early in its work.[2]

The BRC was composed of eight members from Technical Services, two from Public Services, including the facilitator, and one from Collection Management and Special Collections. Both library faculty and support staff were represented, as well as all TSD departments. One of the keys to the success of the BRC was the use of a facilitator from the Facilitators Team. The facilitator's role was essential to the work of the group, guiding the committee so that they could work efficiently through the many facets of the review process. The facilitator used a number of tools to stimulate and guide the BRC's discussions and thought processes.

METHODOLOGY

The BRC used data analysis, organizing principles, and a set of themes and goals in reviewing the reports of the working groups. The BRC held discussions with individual working groups to further clarify sections of their reports and to garner additional information as necessary. Discussions were also held with staff from across the libraries in order to hear recommendations and concerns about the reorganization of Technical Services.

After reviewing the detailed documents of the working groups, the BRC developed flowcharts of the division's work to get an overall picture of what was done in what areas and to capture the redundancies in the current organization. To expand the understanding of the redundancies of effort, the BRC traced the flow of materials from one department to another on the division's floor plans.

The BRC used facilitation tools and exercises at nearly all of its meetings. One especially useful tool was the Merlin Exercise.[3] The BRC applied this visioning tool by asking the group to first imagine what the organization would look like five years into the future. The group then worked backward to the present, identifying key strategies and goals that needed to be met along the way in order to arrive successfully at the desired future. Identifying where the division was going and what it would look like when it got there gave an important framework to the group's continued work.

At the same time the BRC was envisioning the following organizing principles:

- The structure will be administratively centralized.
- The structure will support a streamlined workflow.
- The structure will rely on a staff that has a broad knowledge base and is cross-trained in multiple activities.
- The structure will be supported by teams that serve to provide leadership and coordination between physically separate production groups and divisions.
- The structure will allocate staff resources to accommodate the work loads.
- The structure will be based on a five-year vision of TSD's future.
- The physical space will affect our administrative structure.
- The structure will not include workflow or procedures in detail.

The BRC created a number of bubble graphs (Figures 4.1–4.3) to illustrate the proposed reorganization of the division. These showed the relationships of newly created production groups (formerly departments), coordinating teams and links from Technical Services out into the larger library organization.

Upon completion of their charge, BRC members wrote Working Paper #6: "Technical Services Division in a Team-Based Learning Organization,"[4] which documents in detail the process described above. The most significant section is highlighted here to show the important lessons learned throughout this endeavor:

> The Blue Ribbon Committee digested and synthesized a tremendous amount of data in the process of developing the proposed structure. Several themes emerged from the study and corresponding goals were affirmed. These themes heavily influenced the BRC in shaping its proposal. Each is summarized below.
>
> First, many of the current procedures are complicated and material passes through many hands. A new structure must promote streamlined procedures and eliminate duplication of effort.
>
> Second, the Committee recognized that TSD tasks require a tremendous amount of expertise—the knowledge and skill set required is

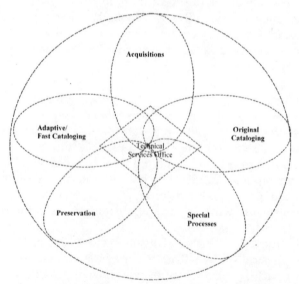

Figure 4.1.   Production Groups and Administrative Office

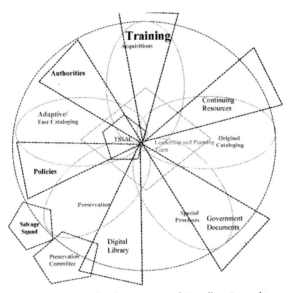

Figure 4.2.   Coordinating Teams and Standing Committees

Production Groups: **Acquiring**

Production Teams:
- Ordering Team
- Continuing Resources Team
- Business Team
- Licensing Team

Production Group Leadership
- Acquiring Production Group Leader (Faculty)
- Production Team Leaders
- Additional members from Teams
- (number to be determined by Production Group)

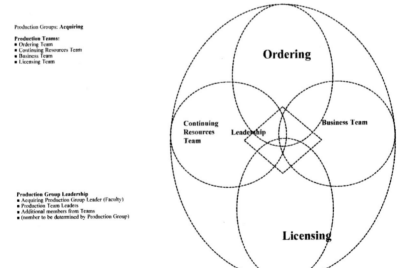

Figure 4.3.   Production Groups: Acquiring

large and multifaceted. Training in basic concepts and routine decision-making is necessary for an effective operation. Furthermore, there must be opportunities for continuing education as the organization and procedures change. Basic learning and on-going development is so intrinsic to the success of Technical Services that the Committee agreed that a training component must be incorporated into the structure.

Third, it was observed that individuals have different skill sets and often specialized skill sets. Specialization is both an advantage and a disadvantage. On the one hand, staffs that specialize know their work and are able to perform tasks well and quickly. On the other hand, specialization can become so narrow that individuals participating in the same work stream are not familiar with the role and the tasks of their colleagues. In other circumstances, job specialization causes processes to result in bottlenecks because the work flows from a larger group to a smaller group or from a faster process to a slower process. To address the issue of specialization, the Committee concluded that the new structure must advocate an environment where staff have a broader knowledge base and are able to perform a wider variety of tasks relating to their work.

Fourth, there need to be improvements in communication about priorities and status of materials within TSD, as well as between TSD and other divisions. The new structure must facilitate communication and collaboration across the organization by bringing together staff that have an interest in specific areas of work.

Fifth, participation in national programs such as the Program for Cooperative Cataloging which supports NACO, SACO, BIBCO, and CONSER, continues to be important. A new structure must promote and provide the widest opportunity for staff to share expertise and participate in these programs.

And sixth, processes in TSD are strongly tied to the Libraries' Integrated Library System (ILS). A new structure must be flexible and able to adapt to changes and opportunities that are brought about by a library system, which provides greater capabilities.

In addition to the themes summarized above, the BRC identified many specific processes and procedures that would need to be explored and addressed in some way. The Committee categorized these activities into four distinct groups: 1) short term recommendations: those that have solutions that can be achieved very quickly, or those that must be addressed urgently; 2) long term recommendations: those that should be addressed after the new ILS is implemented, or require more time to investigate; 3) policy recommendations: those that affect policies for which library-wide input is needed; 4) recommendations for PITs: those that will require a Process Improvement Team to examine the current procedures and the desired outcome. These recommendations have been forwarded to the TSD Council, the leadership body before the reorganization, so that work could begin in updating processes and procedures.[5]

One of the last tasks accomplished by the BRC was the creation of the Transition Team. The committee recognized that while it had accomplished its work, the process of carrying out the Blue Ribbon Committee's recommendations and fleshing out the reorganization (putting legs on it, so to speak) remained. The Transition Team was created to carry the BRC energy on to the next level.

TRANSITION TEAM

The Transition Team's charge was to update all position descriptions, devise a process for populating the newly approved positions, and establish a framework for a larger, fully functional divisional team structure, that is, set up coordinating teams. The work of the team was complex and time consuming, requiring about six months to complete—from fall 2001 to spring 2002. The team consisted of eleven members, and incorporated library faculty and clerical staff, as well as a facilitator who supported the work of the team. Eight members came from Technical Services, including the TSD director; one was the head of the Library Personnel and Budget Office; one was the director of the Planning and Administrative Services Division; and one was a Public Services librarian. The new team structure for TSD was gradually implemented between spring and summer of 2002. Specific details in this process are described below.

DEVELOPING POSITION DESCRIPTIONS

The first step in this process was to review the BRC's staffing recommendations for each of the newly proposed production groups. In some cases, the total number of positions for a group was increased or reduced. In others, the recommended ranks were raised or lowered, based on tasks that a person in a particular job would be expected to perform. Since staff were assured that nobody would be left without a position, the team was careful to keep that promise. Positions vacant in 2000 were purposely left unfilled while the program review was underway. They were left open for the BRC and the Transition Team to maintain as much flexibility as possible as they carried out their work. As it turned out, the number of positions ultimately approved at the end of the process was actually higher than the total number of staff TSD employed at the time. These vacant positions were slowly filled over the next few years, as the needs became pressing and the libraries' budget allowed.

With the assistance of the head of Personnel and Budget, the team proceeded to update job descriptions for existing positions and draft descriptions for new positions. The goal was to create clear and accurate position descriptions, which were standardized and consistent throughout the TSD, and also were detailed enough for each specific case. To speed up the process, subcommittees were appointed to work on different categories of job descriptions. The drafts were then brought before the Transition Team for further revisions and final approval. During this process, the team also identified behaviors, attitudes, and competencies all TSD employees are expected to have or attain in the context of the new team environment. This was spelled out in a document called *Common Expectations of All Staff,*[6] which accompanied all job descriptions and also became a part of the libraries' faculty and staff Performance Review Development (PRD) process.

STAFF PLACEMENT PROCESS

Once all the job descriptions were updated and the timeline for advertising and filling them established, the team moved on to the next tasks: to create a smooth, fair process for reassigning staff and to establish selection criteria. It should be pointed out that the BRC did not envision this transition as a typical "job application" process, but more an opportunity for staff to express interest in different positions for which they were qualified. Many staff, however, viewed it as a job application process, and this caused a great deal of stress.

Staff was directed to submit Expression of Interest forms for each position in writing, describing why they were interested in a specific position, what relevant skills and experience they had, and in what other positions they were also interested, in their order of preference. The Transition Team provided documentation[7] to help staff through the process. This step was necessary because one-to-one correlations between the old and the new positions did not exist in every instance.

Some positions were upgraded to a higher rank and required a combination of skills that were not unique to just one person.

In an effort to widen the pool of possible candidates and select the best-qualified people, the Transition Team chose to open all positions to every staff member within the libraries and not limit them to TSD staff only. Job descriptions were advertised by category, starting with production group leaders, followed by faculty, and finally proceeding through the ranks of the clerical staff. The staff expressed their interest for the positions in the order in which they were advertised. Due to the fact that in the course of the program review several opportunities for advancement had been created, there was an element of anticipation for the staff who recognized themselves as likely candidates for those positions.

Five placement committees were created, one for each rank of positions. Each committee was chaired by a member of the Transition Team and consisted of members from the libraries at large. Working independently of each other and taking into account the preference of each staff member, they proceeded to match each position with the best-qualified candidate.

Every candidate for a production group leader position had to go through a two-part interview process: an open presentation to all interested library staff, followed by a question-and-answer session, and a formal interview session with the placement committee. Other faculty and staff were not interviewed, unless more than one fully qualified candidate had expressed an interest in a position. In fact, out of over sixty people, only two were interviewed.

Upon examining candidates' expressions of interest for their assigned rank, each placement committee submitted its written recommendations to the TSD director, who completed the process. In addition to reviewing (and in most cases approving) the recommendations of placement committees, the TSD director also resolved some of the problems in the process. Placements were found for a few individuals who either had not applied for any jobs or did not get the positions for which they had expressed interest. Finally, all placement results were announced to the TSD staff.

It is important to emphasize that throughout this process, not only were there no job losses, there were also no demotions. The process was planned in such a way that if candidates were assigned to positions with a lower rank than previously held, for which they did not apply, the candidates retained their existing rank and salary. Those who applied for a higher ranking position received a pay raise. Due to budgetary constraints, raises came several months later but were retroactive. It is also important to note that 28 percent of the staff received promotions and upgrades as a direct result of the reorganization.

PUTTING A PLAN FOR A LARGER STRUCTURE IN PLACE

In addition to redesigning individual jobs within TSD, the BRC recommended that a number of coordinating teams be established. These teams were created to ensure collaboration, communication, and coordination in designing and implementing policies and processes involving various TSD and occasionally other library groups. Each of these teams was expected to function as a self-managed team and operate under the principles of shared decision making and consensus, where each team member would be responsible for leadership in solving problems and improving processes. Team membership was to be voluntary and temporary, on a two- to three-year rotational schedule.

The proposed teams were

- Authorities Coordinating Team
- Cataloging Policy Coordinating Team
- Continuing Resources Coordinating Team
- Federal Documents Processing Coordinating Team
- Training Coordinating Team
- Digital Library Coordinating Team

The Authorities and the Cataloging Policy Coordinating Teams would address TSD's policies, procedures, workflows, and training issues and be populated only by TSD staff. The membership of the other four coordinating teams would consist of interested members from TSD and the rest of the libraries. The Transition Team drafted charges and recommended membership by type of position for all the teams and sent a call for volunteers. Once formed, the teams were expected to work with facilitators to select their chairs, gel as teams, review their charges, and develop their work plans. It took team members on average six months to become comfortable in their new role within the new environment.

In addition to the six core teams listed above, one more team was established: the TSD Planning and Leadership Coordinating Team (PLCT). This team was charged with guiding the division; planning, introducing, and coordinating TSD's programs, policies, and services; collaboratively solving problems facing the division; and exchanging ideas and information. The PLCT membership included the TSD director, production group leaders, and coordinating team leaders.

THEORY VERSUS PRACTICE: WHAT TSD LOOKS LIKE NOW

Production Groups

As recommended by the BRC, the newly reorganized TSD was to consist of five production groups:

- Acquisitions
- Adaptive Cataloging
- Original Cataloging
- Special Processes
- Preservation

Two months after the Transition Team began its work, it became obvious that the Adaptive Cataloging and the Special Processes Production Groups should be merged into a single Adaptive Cataloging/Database Management (ACDM) Production Group. This made sense since these two groups were the smallest and required a similar base of knowledge. By reducing the number of production group leaders by one, the Transition Team was able to use this position and salary to fund urgent staffing needs in other TSD areas, and to also create more leadership opportunities for clerical staff. Two staff positions were upgraded to team leader positions, one for the Adaptive Cataloging team and another for the Database Management team, to assist with the management of the newly merged group.

Coordinating Teams

During the process of writing charges for coordinating teams, the Transition Team realized that team membership needed to be reduced in every instance, from eight or nine members, as proposed by the BRC, down to five to seven. Due to regular job demands, it became difficult to recruit volunteers for some of the teams. Creation of the Digital Library Coordinating Team was postponed at the time and is still on hold, two and a half years later. However, other library-wide groups were formed to address this need.

The Training Coordinating Team was perceived as the most urgently needed of all coordinating teams. The Transition Team formed an Interim Training Team, as a precursor to the Training Team. Its charge was to identify training needs and resources for TSD staff, create a description of TSD core competencies, coordinate staff training among TSD production groups, and support the libraries' Learning Curriculum. The team was active between March and December 2002, when it completed its charge and announced its findings and recommendations in the "Interim Training Team Report."[8] The PLCT made an effort to form a new, permanent Training Coordinating Team but postponed formation of the team due to the lack of qualified volunteers. To ensure that staff training be continuous and timely, the PLCT took that responsibility upon itself.

Since the time of the release of the BRC's recommendations, the Authorities, Cataloging Policy, Continuing Resources, and Federal Documents Processing Coordinating Teams have formed and developed their work plans based on their charges and have met their goals with varying degrees of success. They collected data, collaborated with library-wide stakeholders, created the needed policies, and conducted training sessions for staff. Team membership continues to be refined as the organization matures and circumstances develop and change.

SUCCESSES AND CHALLENGES

During the implementation of the reorganization, a campus space planner was consulted with regard to the physical arrangement of people, equipment, and space within the division. Due to environmental and budgetary constraints, some teams were temporarily separated geographically from each other. For example, one group leader was located one hundred feet across the floor from her team. One group remains divided due to space limitations, with half its members on the second floor and the other half in the basement. There was also a delay relocating telephones for people who had moved to their new team locations. Using existing furniture, the physical reallocation of the space was arranged to allow most staff more spacious or more private work areas.

Teamwork within an organization that retains some elements of hierarchy poses an ongoing challenge for a number of staff. As the TSD works toward achieving consensus and practicing shared decision making, staff sometimes struggle to understand what parameters and boundaries structure these efforts. In many ways the libraries' administrative reporting structure retains hierarchical elements, while team structures encourage staff to share ideas for continuous improvement, try new approaches, and take on new challenges. Staff have not yet reached a common understanding of what "teamwork" really is. On the positive side, opportunities have been created for staff input on their work, workflows, and processes through participation in coordinating teams and production groups. There are more opportunities for wider staff input into decisions both small and large, such as providing feedback on the development of the libraries' new strategic plan, or participation in library-wide groups. Some staff rose to meet the changes with enthusiasm and energy, while others would prefer to be told what to do as they had been in the past.

Today, as a result of the reorganization, more staff participate in leadership opportunities throughout TSD. The Original Cataloging Production Group (OCPG) has the highest concentration of library faculty members within TSD, twelve out of sixteen members. This group has been experimenting with rotating team leadership as recommended by the BRC in order to provide library faculty the opportunity to take part in formal leadership. Each of the three teams within OCPG selects their own team leader and determines their rotation schedule. This experiment has produced mixed results and will be reevaluated.

In the course of reorganization, following the library-wide changes mentioned earlier, TSD strove to improve its work culture. Formal leaders, especially the recently promoted ones, and their staff worked hard to establish the kind of relationship desirable in the new environment, where nurturing, respect, and collegiality are a norm. To resolve various personnel issues, some leaders have tapped into the UM campus resources such as professional counseling and workshops on developing personnel skills.

Reorganization has brought forth several workflow changes. One was to transfer processing of purchase plan books from Acquisitions to Adaptive Cataloging. This team was already responsible for copy cataloging of monographs and had the necessary skills for the task. Prior to reorganization, serial issues were added to the catalog in the Catalog Management unit. Now, these are bar-coded in Acquisitions and forwarded to the End Processing Team for labeling. TSD is also in the process of adjusting cataloging workflow for continuing resources. Traditionally, this cataloging was performed in the OCPG; now, simple copy cataloging has been moved into Acquisitions along with two staff to handle the work. To help them master necessary new skills, OCPG serials specialists offered a series of training sessions to Acquisitions staff and made themselves available for follow-up sessions and questions. This allowed OCPG to focus its energy and expertise on the more challenging titles.

There are success stories throughout the TSD for staff who seized the opportunity to advance, show initiative in trying new things, practice their leadership skills, and expand their learning. For example, a very capable staff member, who originally worked as an entry-level technician on very routine tasks, was unsure if she would be seriously considered for the position in which she was interested. She sought out her supervisor's advice on whether to even attempt it, because she thought she could try only for the next higher rank. Reassured that all the positions were indeed open to all who qualified, she made her bid for a position three ranks higher and was successful. After receiving extensive cataloging training, she now performs tasks comparable to those faculty librarians perform. She was also given an opportunity to put her excellent computer skills to a good use by serving as a point of contact for information technology–related questions and problems. She became a web master for her production group and attended an XML workshop.

On the other hand, some staff members had a great deal of difficulty accepting the reorganization and adjusting to it and took another approach. A few did not bid on any positions at all, knowing they would not lose their place in the libraries. They left it up to the TSD director to place them in a position appropriate for their qualifications, fully aware that they might end up in a job different from the one they did previously. For example, one staff person did not bid on her old position, which had been lowered in rank. If she had, she would have lost the high rank that she wanted to keep. In this case, the salary was not a factor in her decision. Since she was fully qualified, she was placed in the reclassified position and retained the rank. Once she leaves, that position will be recruited at the lower rank.

Environmental, leadership, and workflow changes continue to present challenges for the TSD staff. Soon after reorganization, the libraries acquired a new integrated library system that was vastly different from the previous one. TSD staff had to adjust to their new job requirements, new environment, and a new ILS within a year and a half. Staff attended numerous in-house training sessions, presented by TSD trainers, on using the new system; on cataloging, as needed by newly promoted staff; and on name and series authority verification for copy cataloging staff. They also participated in several training sessions taught by the libraries' Staff Learning and Development staff. The TSD staff deserves a lot of credit for overcoming this formidable learning curve.

ASSESSMENT OF TEAM PROGRESS

The TSD staff participated in two assessment processes during 2003 and 2004. The first survey, the "Individual-Team-Organization (ITO) Survey,"[9] was administered in-house as part of an ongoing study of teams in the libraries. This assessment was conducted by the assistant dean for Organizational Development. The second survey, the "Organizational Culture and Diversity Assessment (OCDA),"[10] was administered library-wide by the university's Industrial and Organizational Psychology Program. Both surveys have provided data on the progress of team development, which have been used to identify areas for further development.

The ITO Survey was administered to members of the production groups and coordinating teams in August 2003. This survey is a tool that looks at three components of an organization: individual members of the organization, teams that make up the organization, and the organization itself. Participants are asked to respond to fifty-two statements divided into three areas: individual, team, and organization. A Likert Scale with the range of 5 (almost always) to 0 (almost never) is used with the statements. A fourth section asks respondents to rank their top five issues that need attention from a list of twenty-six terms such as leadership, communication, risk-taking, and job satisfaction.

A valuable use of this survey has been to gather baseline data on the development of the TSD teams. The size of membership ranges from the smallest, nine, to the largest, twenty-two, for the production groups. For the coordinating teams, the range of membership is from five to nine. Overall, the return rate for both sets of teams was 65 percent.

A number of areas are noted positively in the survey results. TSD staff have a clear sense of their jobs and goals individually as well as a team, find their work meaningful, and feel their team has an important function in the libraries. Overall, TSD staff enjoy working in the libraries and are happy to contribute to the organization's mission and goals.

As ITO Survey results have indicated, there is room for continued growth in creating effective practices in decision making and problem solving. The issue of time management is noteworthy. Staff do not feel they are able to give careful consideration to their work because of demands for their time for other things such as meetings and committee work. Another key issue identified is receiving recognition for accomplishments whether individually or as a team.

The OCDA was administered to all library staff in May 2004. This survey was first used in 2000, so the 2004 survey was especially important to gauge what had changed in the libraries' culture over the past four years. This assessment was "designed to measure employees' individual attitudes and beliefs, the Libraries' organizational culture, and current management practices and policies as they relate to diversity."[11] What is also significant about the 2004 survey is that the TSD teams had been in place for two years. The participation rate of all staff in this survey was 71.1 percent, with 23.4 percent of survey respondents coming from TSD.

The overall results of the OCDA show that the libraries have a positive work environment for diversity, and the organization is a place that values and supports diversity. It is a place where teamwork is valued, supported, and effective. Staff are committed to the organization and perceive a fairness in their interpersonal treatment by supervisors. There are, however, more distinctions among the libraries' five divisions in analysis of the data. Currently, staff in each division are reviewing the final report for this survey to identify areas for further development. Some preliminary review indicates that the areas of team development and support will warrant attention in TSD.

CONCLUSION

Library faculty and staff in the TSD embarked on a comprehensive review of workflows and processes in 2000. The review resulted in a number of changes that have addressed ways to improve service to both internal and external customers. New workgroups and teams, new leaders, reorganized space, and shifts in decision-making practices are just a few but very significant outcomes of the review. This process took a great deal of hard work and was very time consuming. However, the TSD is now in a position where continuous improvement is the norm. Continual assessment occurs within teams and also throughout the organization via tools such as the OCDA. The results of these assessments are examined carefully for their implications within the TSD, and future assessments will be conducted to further examine the results of the reorganization efforts.

Some of the lessons learned throughout this process have been easy, while others have been more difficult. What we now know is that

- Change must be continuous. Assessment is key for testing how you are doing and identifying strategies for improvements.
- Patience is critical. Everyone responds to change differently. Communication must be constant, consistent, and clear.
- Learning is extremely important. Whether spontaneous or organized, learning should be ongoing. Supporting the development of skills for decision making, risk taking, and team building is critical.
- The processes used to develop a new structure are as important as the results. Engaging all staff in a major effort like this means they have a stake in the final outcome. Staff may not like all decisions that are made, but they must have an opportunity to share their ideas and concerns.
- Give staff credit for their hard work. Reminding them regularly of the value of their contribution to the great whole is important.

Without question, the program review was needed. It was hard work for all. The results outweigh all else. As the libraries and TSD continue to grow and evolve, the staff are becoming accustomed to thinking critically about what they are doing and why. In that sense, the staff have truly become a part of the learning organization.

NOTES

1. Charles Lowry, "Team Management: The Vision of a Team-Based Learning Organization" (Working Paper #1, June 26, 2000). www.lib.umd.edu/PUB/team_management.html (accessed March 1, 2005).

2. Blue Ribbon Committee, "Technical Services Division in a Team-Based Learning Organization" (Working Paper #6, Appendix A, University Libraries, University of Maryland, College Park, last revised September 17, 2001). www.lib.umd.edu/TSD/workingpaper6_appA-C.html (accessed March 1, 2005).

3. Robert M. Fulmer and Solange Perret, "The Merlin Exercise: Future by Forecast or Future by Invention?" *The Journal of Management Development* 12, no. 6 (1993): 44–52.

4. TSD Blue Ribbon Committee, "Technical Services Division in a Team-Based Learning Organization" (Working Paper #6, University Libraries, University of Maryland, College Park, September 14, 2001). www.lib.umd.edu/TSD/workingpaper6_ptA.html (accessed March 1, 2005).

5. TSD Blue Ribbon Committee, "Technical Services Division in a Team-Based Learning Organization" (Working Paper #6, Section III, "Findings," University Libraries, University of Maryland, College Park, last revised September 22, 2001). www.lib.umd.edu/TSD/workingpaper6_ptA.html#find (accessed March 1, 2005).

6. TSD Transition Team, "Common Expectations of All Staff" (University Libraries, University of Maryland, College Park, October 31, 2001). www.lib.umd.edu/TSD/PROGRAMREV/expectations.html (accessed March 1, 2005).

7. TSD Transition Team, "Reorganization Process of the Technical Services Department" (University Libraries, University of Maryland, College Park, last revised October 29, 2002). www.lib.umd.edu/TSD/reorganization.html (accessed March 1, 2005). Specific documents to review include

- "Expression of Interest/Call for Applications—Guidelines, Instructions, Schedules," www.lib.umd.edu/TSD/PROGRAMREV/guidelines.pdf (accessed March 1, 2005).
- "Expression of Interest Form," www.lib.umd.edu/TSD/PROGRAMREV/eioform.doc (accessed March 1, 2005).
- "FAQ for Expression of Interest in TSD Positions," www.lib.umd.edu/TSD/PROGRAMREV/transition_faq.html (accessed March 1, 2005).

8. Interim Training Team, "Interim Training Team Final Report" (University Libraries, University of Maryland, College Park, January 2003). www.lib.umd.edu/TSD/itt_final.html (accessed March 1, 2005).

9. Sue Baughman, "Individual-Team-Organization (ITO) Survey" (University Libraries, University of Maryland, College Park, February 2005). www.lib.umd.edu/groups/learning/orgdev.html (accessed March 1, 2005).

10. Paul Hanges, Lisa Leslie, and Kirsten Keller, "The University of Maryland Libraries' Organizational Climate and Culture Survey: Final Report" (University Libraries, University of Maryland, College Park, January 2005). www.lib.umd.edu/groups/learning/reports/2004ocdasurvey.pdf (accessed March 1, 2005).

11. Hanges, Leslie, and Keller, "The University of Maryland Libraries' Organizational Climate and Culture Survey," 4.

Chapter 5

Long Live the Team! Factors in the Longevity and Success of a Semiautonomous Work Team

Sarah L. Shreeves, Stephanie Hartman, and Elke Piontek-Ma

The long-term success of a work team hinges on many factors including training, communication, assessment, and organizational support. Perhaps the most crucial factor is commitment to the team by team members themselves. Team activities such as assessment of the efficacy of team activities and attendance to working styles of team members are key to sustaining a high level of commitment from its members. Presented within the context of research on the success and longevity of work teams, this chapter examines the ten-year history of a semiautonomous work team within the Massachusetts Institute of Technology Libraries. The authors identify the key factors in its continuing success and how these have affected its longevity. In particular, the chapter describes team members' efforts to build continuity and a stable team structure and outlines the results and benefits of these efforts.

The success of a work team hinges on many factors, including shared objectives and goals, adaptability, assessment, and a sense of cohesion and mutual trust. But do these same factors contribute to the longevity of a work team? How does the success of a work team feed its longevity? This chapter examines the ten-year history of a semiautonomous work team within the Massachusetts Institute of Technology (MIT) Libraries to identify the key factors in its continuing success and examines how these have affected its longevity. Presented within the context of previously published research on success factors and longevity of work teams, we identify the activities and behaviors that have been crucial to the success of the team. In particular, this chapter describes team members' efforts to build a stable team structure that promotes continuity and success in terms of both performance and team cohesion over time and through multiple staff changes.

We should make three explanatory notes before we begin. The first is that when we speak of a team we are using Cohen and Bailey's definition: "Work teams are continuing work units responsible for producing goods or services. Their membership is typically stable, usually full-time, and well-defined."[1] The second note is that the authors are all either past or current members of the team described in this chapter. As such, we are sharing our experiences and reflections, and although these can be understood within the findings of the literature on teams, neither are they generalizable nor should they be taken as the results of a rigorous research study. We present these in the hopes that our experiences will inform others interested in how teams can succeed over time, and to offer a specific example of a team that has survived for over ten years. Third, for clarity's sake, we use "we" to refer to the authors, and "team" to refer to the work team discussed here as far as we are able.

BACKGROUND

Founded in 1994, the Dewey and Humanities Processing Team is a semiautonomous technical services (or local processing) team of six members—five support staff and one academic professional (the supervisor)—working within two public service divisions of the MIT Libraries, the Dewey Library for Management and Social Sciences and the Humanities Library. The mission of the Dewey and Humanities Processing Team is to provide all library users and staff with accurate and timely processing of library materials and maintenance of the online catalog and other online resources to support the accessibility of library materials in all formats as well as the professional services of the MIT Libraries.

The team was formed through the merger of the existing local processing units in the Dewey and Humanities Libraries. A combination of circumstances including staffing shortages and the merger of the administration of the two libraries made it possible to introduce a new organizational structure for the processing units. At the time of the merger the Dewey processing office had three full-time support staff positions, one of which was unfilled, one half-time support staff position, and one vacant supervisor (academic professional) position. The Humanities processing unit had a full-time supervisor (also an academic professional) and one full-time support staff member. With the merger of the two units the Humanities supervisor split his time equally between Dewey and Humanities, and the Dewey supervisor position was eliminated. The half-time position at Dewey was combined with a half-time position at Humanities to create one full-time position that also worked at both libraries.

At the time of the merger, two staff members were long-time employees of the MIT Libraries, but the majority had been hired since 1992. One employee left during the formation period, and a new staff member was hired explicitly as a member of the team. Job descriptions from that point on have included a description of the team environment and highlight collaborative skills as an important aspect of each position. Over the team's ten-year history, there have been three team supervisors, two of whom were hired from within the team. In total, twenty individuals have worked in the team over the last ten years; fourteen of these were recruited after the team's formation. On average, each of the six positions has had four incumbents, and the average number of years in a position is currently two and a half years. Table 5.1 outlines the personnel changes over the past ten years.

The process to move from a unit of individuals to a cohesive and high-performing team took approximately two years. During that period the continued support of the Dewey and Humanities Libraries administration was crucial. It is difficult to judge when staff members outside the team accepted this new entity, but as more and more had positive experiences with the team and the way it worked, acceptance grew steadily.

Table 5.1. Staffing History of the Dewey and Humanities Processing Team (1994–2004)

	Supervisor/ Team Leader	Humanities Collections Asst.	Humanities Journals/Dewey Binding Asst.	Dewey Journals Asst.	Dewey Serials Asst.	Dewey Collections Asst.
1994 (Original Team)	TM1 (longtime employee)	TM 2 (longtime employee)	TM 3 (started in May 1994)	TM 4 (started in May 1992)	TM 5 (started in Sept. 1994)	TM 6 (July 1992– Fall 1994) TM 7 (started in Dec. 1994)
1995						
1996	TM 1 leaves TM 4 moves (Mar.)			TM 8 (started in Apr.) Tm 9 (started in Aug.)		
1997		TM 2 leaves, TM 8 moves summer				
1998					TM 5 leaves, TM 10 (started in Oct.)	
1999			TM 3 leaves (summer), TM 7 begins (fall)			TM 11(started in Dec.)
2000	TM 4 leaves Nov.), TM 10 moves (Dec.)	TM 8 leaves (May) TM 12 (started in Aug.)	TM 7 leaves (June), TM 14 (started in Sept.)	TM 9 leaves (June), TM 13 (started in Aug.)		

2001					
TM 10 (permanent appointment, May)			TM 15 (June–Sept.)		

2002					
	TM 12 leaves (Nov.)	TM 14 leaves (July), TM 17 (started in Sept.)		TM 16 (started in Jan.)	TM 11 leaves Dec.

2003					
					TM 18 (started in Apr.)

2004					
	TM 13 moves (Jan.), TM 13 leaves (June), TM 20 (started in Oct.)			TM 19 (started in Mar.)	

Number of Staff Staff Members in Position					
3	5	4	5	4	4
Number of Moves within the Team					
2	2	1			
Average Number of Years in Position per Incumbent					
3.67	2	2.5	2	2.5	2.5

RESEARCH ON GROUP SUCCESS AND LONGEVITY

How do we define success? What does a successful team look like? The metaliterature reviews and analyses of Paris, Salas, and Cannon-Bowers[2] and Guzzo and Dickson[3] have summarized a wide range of success indicators for high performance as well as the traits and competencies needed to reach them. We are particularly drawn to Sundstrom, De Meuse, and Futrell's definition:

> We favor a broad definition [of an effective team] that accounts for members' satisfaction and the group's future prospects as a work unit by incorporating *team viability*. At a minimum, this entails members' satisfaction, participation, and willingness to continue working together. A more demanding definition might add cohesion, inter-member coordination, mature communication and problem-solving, and clear norms and roles—all traditionally identified with team maturity. *Performance* means acceptability of output to customers within or outside the organization who receive team products, services, information, decisions, or performance events (such as presentations or competitions) [emphasis theirs].[4]

Following these summaries and drawing on our own experience in the team, we have specifically identified the following to be indicators of this team's success:

- Team cohesiveness is strong among team members.[5]
- Mutual trust exists among team members.[6]
- Open communication exists within the team and with staff and units outside of the team.[7]
- Performance goals are met and exceeded.[8]
- Team members have an interest in and are involved in the environment outside the immediate team.[9]
- The team can adapt to a changing environment.[10]

Each of these appears repeatedly in the literature as a defining characteristic of an effective team.

A significant portion of the literature focused on "project teams," that is, teams with a limited life cycle.[11] Group longevity has not been an important factor in this facet of the research. However, even research on work teams has tended to ignore temporal effects on the development of teams. In 1986, McGrath called for more research on the temporal patterns of work groups.[12] Cohen and Bailey repeated that call in 1997 and noted that the lack of longitudinal studies is a significant gap in the research on teams.[13] Schippers et al. also note the lack of longitudinal studies.[14] Most recently Arrow et al. conducted a literature review of studies that included a temporal perspective (of any kind) on small groups and concluded that while an impressive amount of research had been conducted, there existed "vast areas of terrain" yet to be explored.[15] Subsequently, there is not yet a good understanding of temporal effects on team effectiveness and performance.

Despite this dearth of research on group longevity, there are a handful of relevant observations from the literature. Katz studied the effect of group longevity (as measured by the average length of time that group members had worked together) on behavior and performance. He found that the optimum amount of time for a group to work together was approximately two to four years. Work groups whose members have worked together longer on average tended to have a reduction in their performance levels, were increasingly isolated from outside sources of new ideas, and grew more complacent.[16] In contrast Schippers et al. found that more homogeneous teams (in terms of age, gender, educational level, and tenure) that had been together longer were more reflexive, that is, explicitly reflected on their goals, strategies, and processes and adapted them accordingly.[17] These authors suggest that these teams have learned to build in communication channels and other organizational strategies to counter a tendency toward isolation. Arrow et al. note that "[c]ontinuity occurs in groups that experience change while maintaining and reenacting consistent patterns and structure."[18]

Throughout the discussion so far we have been careful not to equate longevity to success. In the team's ten-year history there have been two specific points when the team could easily have been disbanded or collapsed, such as when the administration of the Dewey and Humanities Libraries was pulled apart in 1998, or when four of the six members left the team in 2000 (see Table 5.1). The team survived in both cases. We suggest that our team's ability to effectively and iteratively reinforce successful participatory behaviors, attitudes, and skills as detailed below, a healthy dose of luck, and the strong support from the administration have contributed to the team's ability to survive over the long term.

SUCCESS FACTORS

So what are these participatory behaviors, attitudes, and skills? We believe that the key success factors for the Dewey and Humanities Processing Team are that

- The entire team participates in the hiring and training of new team members;
- The team is actively aware of the working styles, personalities, and needs of the individual team members, and team activities are adjusted as needed;
- Decisions (including hiring of new members and goal setting) are made by the consensus of the entire team;
- Team training is conducted by the team internally;
- All team members are cross-trained in each others' responsibilities at both the Dewey and Humanities Libraries;
- Goal setting and assessment of the team's performance (both external and internal) are conducted regularly by the team as a whole; and
- Project management leadership and responsibility are rotated among all team members.

Underlying each of these activities and behaviors are the core principles of open communication and flexibility. We do not discuss these as separate behaviors because they are threaded throughout the discussion below.

The remainder of the chapter is devoted to discussing each of these factors. We describe each of these activities and then discuss the effects they have on our team's success and long-term viability.

HIRING AND INCORPORATING NEW TEAM MEMBERS

What We Do

All team members participate in the hiring process from the beginning to the end. When a position is vacant, the team first reviews the job description to make sure the responsibilities are correct. The descriptions are often tweaked and modified to keep workflows current and to shift responsibilities within the team. The team reviews the resumes as they arrive and determines who will be interviewed, what the interview will look like, and what questions will be asked. While the supervisor does tend to make contact with the interviewees, schedules the interviews (a sometimes onerous process given the need to schedule time with six team members), and handles the administrative details of the search, all team members participate in the substantive portion of the interview. At the end of the interviews, the team discusses the interviewees and comes to a decision about whom to hire. This is not an inconsequential process, as the team uses consensus to reach decisions. The consensus decision-making style is discussed further below, but we note that hiring decisions have generally been the most difficult to make. Once a decision has been made, the supervisor shifts the offer process to the human resources office and contacts the unsuccessful interviewees.

When the new hire arrives, all team members share the responsibility for incorporating and training the new teammate. Training activities are discussed further below, but generally one or two team members have the direct responsibility for training the new hire. In addition the team conducts team-training activities. Recently, the team has decided that each member would spend one-on-one time with the new hire to explain his or her own job in more detail and so that old and new members could get to know one another better.

What Are the Effects?

The overall effect of the hiring and incorporation process is a sense of shared responsibility for the team as an entity in itself as well as an opportunity for the reflective activities as described by Schippers et al.[19] Reviewing the job descriptions gives the team an opportunity to examine and revise workflows to improve performance. It also offers an opportunity for team members to have some task variety and to engage new challenges as the team can shift responsibilities among members when a vacancy occurs. As the team reviews resumes together, members share their thoughts on what—beyond experience—they are looking for in a new team member. What kind of gaps in the team need to be filled? The interviews themselves allow the team to speak about themselves to an outsider and to express their pride in being part of a team. The shared training process ensures a *natural* progression of incorporating and welcoming the new team member and reinforcing a sense of membership among everyone.

As noted above, the decision-making process itself is the most difficult, but often the most rewarding, part of the hiring process. It can take a substantial amount of time—as long as two days of discussion spread out over a week—to come to a consensus on a candidate, particularly when there are two or more strong ones. The consensus process is discussed in more detail later in the chapter, but suffice it to say that the team has consistently found this process well worth the time and effort spent. The discussions often uncover issues with team performance and dynamics not previously addressed and in the end have brought greater team cohesion out of struggles to make these important and difficult decisions.

This process has worked particularly well when the team is handling a single vacancy and has a core of team members who have had tenure of a year or more. However, even during periods of substantial turnover, the team has been able to maintain continuity, that is the team structures and processes have stayed intact. The team has been lucky in that at least one anchor—a longstanding team member with experience, knowledge, and leadership skills—has been in place to ensure stability throughout periods of substantial turnover. For example, in 2000, the team witnessed unprecedented turnover, with three veteran members (two with three and one with six years of experience) and the team supervisor (with six years of team experience and eight years in the processing unit) all leaving within the space of seven months (see Table 5.1). Their departure left some very big holes to fill. Fortunately for the survival of the team, a member with three years of experience on the team filled the supervisor position and had the expertise, knowledge, and, most importantly, team development skills to stabilize the reconstituted team. We are uncertain that the team would survive a substantial turnover without a remaining anchor.

ACTIVE AWARENESS OF PERSONALITY
AND WORKING STYLES

What We Do

The team's initial formation period was rocky. Most members had been brought together through the merging of the two local processing units, and not the current hiring process. We were suddenly charged to think and approach our work in a new way. It was at this point that the team began to learn the value of understanding personality and working styles and what effect that understanding could have on the team itself.

During the team training that occurred in the team's formation period (1994–1996), personality and working style instruments were administered to all team members (including the Myers-Briggs Type Indicator and the DiSC Behavioral Style Indicator instruments). There were skeptics in the group regarding the usefulness of these tools, but in the end the results did show some interesting trends. In particular, they illustrated that the team had few strong communicators. Those who were in this category were essentially the team's motivators and had an uphill battle working to increase the group's optimism, sense of cohesion, trust, and communication. Discussing the results of these instruments allowed the team to confront this imbalance of personalities and to find a middle ground between the differing personalities.

Since this initial experience with these instruments, the team has tried to maintain an active awareness of the personality and working styles of its members and to maintain a balance between differing styles. The team uses personality and working style instruments, but it has been important to also include discussions about these issues at the regular team meetings, during project planning, and particularly during the hiring process.

What Is the Effect?

Active awareness of personality and working style has allowed the team to understand where its members' strengths and weaknesses lie and to think creatively about how best to go about our internal team work and with interactions with outside staff. The team is made up of a diverse set of personalities: detail-oriented people, *big picture* people, creative types, skeptics, starters, and finishers. Understanding these traits and styles has been absolutely crucial when planning projects and workflows. Personal awareness of one's own personality type or working style has allowed members to challenge themselves by taking on roles they might not be comfortable in—for example, a big picture person learning how to plan a project, or an introvert leading a team meeting or serving on a system-wide committee.

While awareness of personalities was crucial during the formation period, it remains critical with each new hire and thus each new iteration of the team. As people come and go from the team, they take or bring new energy, experiences, and attitude. Questions asked of the candidate are often directed at understanding a candidate's working style and personality, and this understanding is of high importance during the decision-making process. Knowing what the team has lost when a team member leaves and when a new team member joins helps to maintain shared awareness of team dynamics.

CONSENSUS BUILDING

What We Do

When the team was formed, we decided that the team decision-making process would be by consensus, that is, coming to a decision as a group. This does not mean that all team members have to agree completely with a decision, but that they can live with and support the decision. The consensus process has been used continuously for all team decisions, but not all decisions individual members make about their work (an important distinction). However, it is used for goal setting, hiring decisions, project planning, and any decision that involves the team as a whole.

The consensus-making process itself can be time intensive. Each member of the team contributes opinions, and the group then seeks to find the common ground. When there is disagreement, the team attempts to work through that decision point using a variety of facilitation and decision-making tools.

What Is the Effect?

As noted earlier, consensus is not always easy, nor is it always quick. It can be an exhausting and excruciating process, and there have been times—particularly in hiring processes—when the team did not think it would survive the process. However, in every case a decision has been made that the entire team could and did support. Team members have found that the process of consensus building and the ability to come to consensus are heavily grounded in trust. Team members do not have to agree with the team's decision, but they must agree to live with and support that decision. This is much easier to do if you trust the judgment and opinions of your colleagues and trust in the decision-making ability of the group as a whole.

The support from all team members is key. For example, even if a new hire was not the first choice of a team member, he or she must agree to support the decision made by the group. This support is shown both internally within the team (training and encouraging the new hire, for instance), as well as externally to other departments and units. The lack of support—even from a single team member—would undermine the trust and open communication built through the consensus process. (This is not to say that the team as a group does not revisit decisions—it does.) The shared responsibility that comes with consensus is crucial to team cohesion, mutual trust, and open communication.

TEAM TRAINING

What We Do

To help with the transition from an individual to a collaborative working style, the group attended several formal team-training sessions in 1994 and 1996 (led by a trainer from the Association of Research Libraries) and continued to attend formal training sessions offered by the MIT Training Office whenever new team members were hired into the group until 2002. Some sessions were only as long as an afternoon, while others were two day or several days over a series of weeks. In 2002, the team decided they needed a different type of training because the sessions offered by MIT focused almost exclusively on building teams and did not address issues of existing teams, such as how to incorporate new members. As the team has been unable to identify any other viable options, the team itself has taken over the team-training functions and has adapted activities and tools from the formal team-training sessions for use in their existing environment.

What Is the Effect?

The formal team-training sessions were especially useful and successful in the beginning stages of the team. These sessions helped team members understand team dynamics (as we outlined in the section on awareness of personality and working styles), how to set goals and measure performance, and techniques for decision making and communication. In addition, the sessions gave the team time away from daily responsibilities to focus on needs and issues within the team.

However, as noted above, as the team has evolved over the last decade, these formal team-training sessions have fallen short of the needs of a mature, established team. Taking over the training functions has added another layer to the "self-managed" aspect of the team. The team has had to be proactive about recognizing team training needs, how to respond to them, and when to take "away time" in the form of one-day retreats.

CROSS-TRAINING

What We Do

Each member of the team is a "specialist" in one or more specific areas, whether journals processing and claiming, order processing, or government documents. However, each team member is also competent in the daily duties of the other team members. Cross-training requires that each team member be not only a trainee but also a trainer. After growing comfortable in the responsibilities of his or her own position, each team member is trained in the basic functions of each of the other team positions by the other team members. The end result is that the journals assistant is proficient in the typical processing of serials, monographs, and orders. The collections assistant can take over journal and serial binding when necessary. In addition, each team member is cross-trained in duties in both their home library (Dewey or Humanities) and the other library.

What Is the Effect?

Cross-training is time- and resource-intensive; it occurs with each new hire, and refresher sessions are offered as well. In addition, as workflow processes change (for example, with the implementation of a new library management system), training needs to be updated and revisited. However, cross-training fosters a team-wide understanding of the responsibilities and problems encountered in each position and how each position relates to the others in the team. Team members tend to gain a greater appreciation for the work other members do. Learning about your teammate's responsibilities allows for opportunities to look at your own responsibilities differently and enhances your problem-solving skills.

Another obvious benefit to cross-training is that it facilitates coverage during vacations, illnesses, and vacancies. Cross-training also means that staff members outside the team do not have to find the "specialist" to ask a question or request a solution to a problem; they can approach any team member, who will respond immediately. Only when higher level skills or knowledge are required will the team member refer the question or problem to the appropriate team member. The result is faster service to the team's constituencies and ultimately better service to the library user.

GOAL SETTING AND TEAM ASSESSMENT

What We Do

The team sets aside time each year to set and prioritize goals for the year and to assess its progress on past goals. Goals include task-oriented ones (moving 20,000 volumes to storage), process-oriented ones (improving communication with other library units), and internally oriented ones (improving communication within the team). They can originate from team members or from other library units or system-wide priorities. As part of the goal setting, team members strategize on how best to meet each goal and who on the team will have responsibility. The team assesses conflicting priorities (for example, when both the Dewey and the Humanities Libraries have resource-intensive projects underway), individual workloads, and the time and resources needed to meet the goals. The goal setting exercise is a consensus-driven process, and the decisions made are revisited throughout the year, particularly as internal and external pressures and priorities shift.

In conjunction with the goal-setting process, the team goes through an annual assessment process similar to the annual performance review of individual staff members (indeed using the same form that is used for individual staff members). While this form is far from perfect for use by a team, it does allow for reflection and evaluation of how well projects and daily responsibilities were performed by the team and the effectiveness of the internal activities and processes. The process includes

- Evaluation of progress toward goals
- Listing of major accomplishments and obstacles to progress
- Appraisal of the team's job knowledge, initiative, and resourcefulness
- Review of the team's communication, organizational, interpersonal, and problem-solving skills

During the assessment process the team tries to distinguish the team's performance and skill level as distinct from the performance and skill level of its individual members—an often difficult task. The team assessment is not formally connected to the performance review of the individual team members.

What Is the Effect?

The goal-setting and assessment activities are built-in periods for reflection, assessment, reorientation, and prioritization and go hand in hand. The goal-setting process allows the team to address problems of conflicting priorities arising from serving two public service units and to reassess activities in areas that may no longer be a priority for the team or the MIT Libraries. Team members will raise concerns about shifting workloads and workflows, and the team can work together to address these disparities. Team goal setting also ensures that every team member endorses the priorities set for the coming year and that the entire team is responsible for meeting those agreed-upon goals.

The annual evaluation allows each team member the opportunity to reflect on and express his or her opinion of how the team is doing, how the team is handling the daily work and projects, and the team's relationships with other units. The team can develop and adopt strategies to respond to perceived problems and gaps in performance.

We should note that goal setting and assessment also occur on a regular basis throughout the year as needed, but the annual process is time set aside explicitly for the team to reflect on its performance and internal processes over the past year and for the next year—reflection that as, Schippers et al. point out, can be an important strategy for a well-performing team.[20]

SHARED LEADERSHIP

What We Do

At the start of this chapter we describe the makeup of the team as five support staff members and one academic professional who has the supervisory responsibility for the team. In practice, while the supervisor does have responsibility for evaluation of individual team members and administrative responsibility for the team as a whole, the person in this position acts as a team leader rather than a supervisor. However, the team leader is not solely responsible for leading the team. The team practices shared leadership, which is mostly expressed through rotated facilitation of team meetings and project management. Any team member can be the manager for a specific project. The project manager is responsible for

- Planning the stages of the project in conjunction with the rest of the team
- Communication with the team and outside staff about the project
- Procuring the necessary supplies and resources for the project
- Training team members, if necessary
- Documentation of procedures
- Statistics management

Examples of such projects include retrospective bar-coding of journals collections and mass storage projects.

Shared leadership is also exhibited in everyday work processes as team members communicate and work with one another to solve problems and alleviate heavy workloads. Team members also participate in system-wide initiatives and committees and communicate information from these activities back to the team.

What Is the Effect?

Project management helps team members develop leadership skills in a supportive environment. First-time project managers will usually have other more experienced team members to mentor them during difficult stages of projects. Once team members develop these skills, they tend to become more active in initiatives and committees across the library system. This ensures that information is flowing into the team from not only the team leaders but other sources as well. Although Katz's research was focused on research and development project teams, he does suggest that information flow is crucial to continued high performance of teams.[21]

An important indicator of how well the team has fostered leadership skills is that the two times the supervisor/team leader position has been vacant since the team began it has been filled by a team member. The team's ability to develop its own leaders has contributed greatly to the team's longevity and success. The MIT Libraries have also benefited: Three additional team members moved into academic professional positions within the system in part because of the leadership (and other) skills they developed on the team.

CONCLUSION

We have outlined the activities, participatory behaviors, and skills that have contributed to the success of the team as well as its longevity. We also want to acknowledge that the support of the administration and staff of the Dewey and Humanities Libraries, as well as the MIT Libraries as a whole, has had an enormous impact on the team over its ten-year history. In particular, when the Dewey and Humanities Libraries were split, the team was allowed to continue to work across the two libraries. The ability of the heads of the Dewey and Humanities Libraries to "share" the team since that point has been crucial to its survival.

We acknowledge that there are some gaps in what we have presented here. For example, we have not discussed in any depth the impact on team dynamics of having an academic professional and supervisor working on the team with five support staff members. The team has never fully explored these dynamics in part because the supervisor works very hard to downplay that role and to allow other team members to participate fully without feeling *supervised*—in a sense acting as an *unleader* as described by Manz and Sims.[22] This, however, is an area that the team should explore more fully.

We have identified what a successful Dewey and Humanities Processing Team looks like and what behaviors and activities have contributed to that success. But what are some of the larger tangible successes? A handful of these are the following:

- The team has been chosen to pilot several activities, including online serials check-in, in part because the team structure can incorporate unexpected activities such as these.
- As noted above, team members have gone on to more responsible positions within the MIT Libraries because of the skills they have developed with the team.
- The team has been asked to consult with other departments within the MIT Libraries about establishing a team.
- The team received the MIT Libraries 2004 Infinite Mile Team Award in the category of Communication and Collaboration.

These successes are primarily the result of the hard work of multiple team members over the past ten years to understand what it means to be a member of a team, to work together to make decisions, to listen and communicate with one another, to share accountability for goals and performance, and to foster an environment of mutual trust.

NOTES

1. Cohen and Bailey, "What Makes Teams Work," *Journal of Management* 23, no. 3 (1997): 242.

2. Carol R. Paris, Eduardo Salas, and Janis A. Cannon-Bowers, "Teamwork in Multi-Person Systems: A Review and Analysis," *Ergonomics* 43, no. 8 (2000): 1054–1055.

3. Richard A. Guzzo and Marcus W. Dickson, "Teams in Organizations: Recent Research on Performance and Effectiveness," *Annual Review of Psychology* 47 (1996): 310–315.

4. Eric Sundstrom, Kenneth P. De Meuse, and David Futrell, "Work Teams: Applications and Effectiveness," *American Psychologist* 43, no. 2 (February 1990): 122.

5. Sundstrom, De Meuse, and Futrell, "Work Teams," 127.

6. Vanessa Urch Druskat and Steven B. Wolff, "Building the Emotional Intelligence of Groups," *Harvard Business Review* 79, no. 3 (March 2001): 82.

7. Sundstrom, De Meuse, and Futrell, "Work Teams," 127.

8. Cohen and Bailey, "What Makes Teams Work," 249–250.

9. Sundstrom, De Meuse, and Futrell, "Work Teams," 122.

10. Holly Arrow, Marshall Scott Poole, Kelly Bouas Henry, Susan Wheelan, and Richard Moreland, "Time, Change, and Development: The Temporal Perspective on Groups," *Small Group Research* 35, no. 1 (February 2004): 87.

11. Cohen and Bailey, "What Makes Teams Work," 242.

12. Joseph E. McGrath, "Studying Groups at Work: Ten Critical Needs for Theory and Practice," in *Designing Effective Work Groups*, ed. Paul S. Goodman and Associates (San Francisco: Jossey-Bass, 1986), 386.

13. Cohen and Bailey, "What Makes Teams Work," 245, 283–284.

14. Michaéla C. Schippers, Deanne N. Den Hartog, Paul L. Koopman, and Janique A. Wienk, "Diversity and Team Outcomes: The Moderating Effects of Outcome Interdependence and Group Longevity and the Mediating Effect of Reflexivity," *Journal of Organizational Behavior* 24 (2002): 798.

15. Arrow et al., "Time, Change, and Development," 74.

16. Ralph Katz, "The Effects of Group Longevity on Project Communication and Performance," *Administrative Science Quarterly* 37, no. 1 (1982): 86, 100–102.

17. Schippers et al., "Diversity and Team Outcomes," 797.

18. Arrow et al., "Time, Change, and Development," 80.

19. Schippers et al., "Diversity and Team Outcomes," 781.

20. Schippers et al., "Diversity and Team Outcomes," 797.

21. Katz, "The Effects of Group Longevity," 101.

22. Charles C. Manz and Henry P. Sims Jr., "Leading Workers to Lead Themselves: The External Leadership of Self-Managing Work Teams," *Administrative Science Quarterly* 32, no. 1 (March 1987): 107.

Chapter 6

Strategic Planning and Organizational Structure in a Team Environment

Marda L. Johnson

The annual planning process at the University of Arizona Library is a complex undertaking and an interteam challenge in coordination. It is an undertaking that provides the library with direction, the teams with organization, and individuals with personal developmental focus. Consequently it lays the foundation for the coming year's work and the library's future.

BACKGROUND

The University of Arizona's Technical Services and Archival Processing (TSAP) Team is composed of three work teams: Ordering and Processing (OPT), Receiving, and Cataloging and Electronic Resources (CERT). There are twenty-two classified staff, two librarians, a team leader, who is also a librarian, and an administrative assistant. The organizational structure is reflected in Figure 6.1.

At this time, the team also draws heavily on student workers, two graduate assistants, and two temporary employees to accomplish the work of the unit.

This group of dedicated personnel is responsible for acquiring, cataloging, physically processing, and maintaining an online catalog of approximately 4,700,000 volumes and over 26,000 serial subscriptions. The team receives over 54,000 new monographs, adds over 38,000 print journal volumes, and maintains over 50,000 links for an electronic journal collection of approximately 25,000 titles.

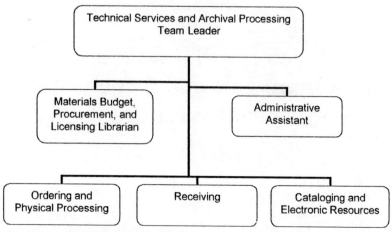

Figure 6.1. TSAP Organizational Chart

Full-time staff are also responsible for the planning, organization, and management of all functions and projects dealing with the acquisitions and processing of resources that support the library's mission. "We connect our customers to information that furthers their education and research goals."[1] This chapter describes how TSAP planned and organized its work processes for the 2004–2005 fiscal year.

STRATEGIC PLANNING

There are three major components to strategic planning at the University of Arizona Library: the university's, the library's, and the individual teams' missions, visions, and goals. One builds on the next to ensure consistency and cohesiveness for providing information to the campus community. While the campus builds an overall program of focused excellence for the university, the library's Strategic Long-Range Planning (SLRP) team concentrates on interpreting this plan to build an organization that supports the coming year's program, while exerting additional effort in identifying new trends in libraries in order to position the library for changes occurring over the next several years. The library's mission—"We connect our customers to information that furthers their education and research goals"[2]—is obviously key to the existence of the Technical Services and Archival Processing Team and provides the foundation of the team's mission in return.

Although TSAP's mission is lengthier in its message, the sentiment expressed builds on the library's mission.

> TSAP provides our internal and external customers with high-quality, accurate, and timely access to information resources. We purchase, license, catalog, and maintain materials in all formats. Staff arranges and describes archival materials and preserves all resources. TSAP investigates and identifies new technologies and processes, enabling us to provide outstanding, cost-effective services that connect our customers to their information resources.[3]

TSAP's mission, along with its vision and goals, are reviewed on an annual basis to determine whether they still fulfill the needs of the library and the community served. It defines the team's purpose for existence in the library and provides broad guidelines within which the team works. (Details on how this mission is accomplished and how a more precise set of goals is built for the year are described later in this chapter.) To better determine what these goals will be, TSAP studies the library's goals, assesses customer needs, and aligns itself with other specialized or cross-functional teams that exist at the time.

In 2004, the SLRP rewrote the library's goals in a broad sense to better reflect the many needs of the library's customers and stakeholders and the library's internal capabilities to perform its mission.

The library's Strategic Goals for 2004–2005 are the following:[4]

1. Customers can identify, quickly obtain, evaluate, and use information that meets their education and research needs.
2. Our strategic stakeholders understand the library's value to the institution and allocate resources accordingly.
3. The library has the capability and flexibility to meet its customer and stakeholder goals in the face of changing environments.

Within each of these goals several strategies are described to assist individual teams in understanding the directions being emphasized by the library, and, in turn, what should be emphasized by teams. Although the strategies cited are not intended to be a comprehensive listing, they do help to focus TSAP when determining what it will be emphasizing for the coming year.

Armed with this information from the university and the library, TSAP begins its own customer needs assessment.

NEEDS ASSESSMENT

TSAP's customers are both internal and external to the library, although its prime functions support the Information Resource (IR) managers (selectors). Their work, in turn, directly supports faculty, students, and other external customers. Each year TSAP staff assess the needs of the primary customers, the IR managers, through various methods. In the past two years a modified focus group approach was used. This method entails outlining the basic work of the area as background information and developing a small, focused set of questions to gauge their perceptions of how TSAP is doing. The questions being used currently are open ended and attempt to draw a full spectrum of comments and reactions. The appendix reflects the questions that TSAP used at the beginning of 2004 in preparation for strategic planning for fiscal year 2004–2005.

As part of this process, the questions were distributed to the Integrative Services (IS) Teams, and a team meeting was scheduled to discuss their issues, comments, and recommendations. Two members of TSAP attended the meetings and took questions, discussed issues, and compiled notes. The results were organized by topic and discussed in detail at the team's offsite strategic planning retreat.

Currently IR manager input is the most reliable reflection of what the external customers (faculty, students, public) need. Occasionally external feedback comes more directly from the library's report card, LibQual, and from questions or purchase requests we receive directly over the web. These "needs" are inserted into the documentation used for deliberation during strategic planning.

The needs fall into three major categories:

1. Big, documented, and needed with real discernible benefit
2. Small, perceived, and usually undocumented
3. New directions not identified by customers

Work teams take responsibility for assessing the feedback from the focus groups by categorizing them and identifying possible approaches for those that need attention. Misperceptions on the part of IS team members are dealt with immediately. These are often solved by being sure IR managers have the latest information about procedural policy. At the end of the planning sessions in the summer of 2004, TSAP responded to all the feedback collected whether it was to answer an outstanding question, create a project around a specific need, or tell teams that we were or are unable to address the issue that was raised. In this way there is a closed circle of compiling requests, assessing the need for solutions, and responding to customers.

CROSS-FUNCTIONAL AND PROJECT TEAMS

In the team environment at the University of Arizona Library, each year brings a bevy of additional cross-functional and project teams working on continuing or short-term issues. For example, most recently there have been two teams formed to research, evaluate, and report on current and future environmental issues that would impact our decision making around access and delivery of information to our customers. Another has analyzed and assessed the method we use to allocate the library's information access budget. The Information Resource Council (IRC) is a standing team responsible for the allocation of the library's information access budget of over $8,000,000. At any one time there could be as few as one to as many as a half dozen other teams that TSAP needs to monitor for the information necessary to inform TSAP in which direction the library is heading.

The primary method used by the library to inform the entire staff about the work of these teams is a system of quarterly library reports. In addition, special cross-functional teams may schedule special open meetings. As issues arise that affect TSAP's current plan or that will affect the planning for the following year, interim adjustments are made in the present plan and projects.

TEAM PROJECTS

The annual team goals for the year are reflected in large part by the projects that TSAP establishes for itself. These projects are in addition to the standard ongoing critical processes of ordering, receiving, cataloging, and maintaining the online catalog. The projects are established through a review of the library's mission, vision, and goals, and TSAP's evaluation of customer needs, at the same time keeping an eye on short-term projects being established for a specific fiscal year. All of the team's projects directly support Library Strategic Goal 1: Customers can identify, quickly obtain, evaluate, and use information that meets their education and research needs. In addition, team projects two and five are also supportive of Library Strategic Goal 3: The library has the capability and flexibility to meet its customer and stakeholder goals in the face of changing environments. As a consequence of planning, TSAP's areas of emphasis in 2004–2005 were the following:[5]

1. Electronic Resources team will institutionalize the related automation processes of electronic holdings, Innovative Interfaces' Electronic Resource Management, and Serials Solutions to ensure that these processes are clearly documented, implemented, and managed. The objective is to provide effective and timely management of all electronic materials accessed by customers. The team will also address several issues that were raised by internal customers that were outlined in TSAP's needs assessment for 2004, including effective placement and handling of orders, cataloging, and linking of electronic materials.

2. Information Access Budget Fund Implementation will be a short-term project with the responsibility to implement the outcomes identified in the Information Access Budget Action Planning Team (IABAPT) reports (a library-wide cross-functional team). The fund structure in SABIO (our online public access catalog) will be changed, and staff in TSAP will have the information they need to correctly assign fund codes. This is a hand-off from IABAPT and needs to be quickly accomplished no later than the end of August to be of value to IR managers and the library for this first fiscal year of the new budget allocation process.

3. Outsourcing Management Improvement will provide a systematic method to assess the quality of the work performed by vendors who provide goods in the form of records and processing for information resources owned by the library. It will entail the evaluation, analysis, documentation, and assessment

of quality standards associated with the processes for all major vendors used within TSAP, including OCLC, BNA, Roswell, and Serials Solutions. We hope to answer the question of both quality and cost/benefit of using outsourcing as a method of providing access information to the library's materials.

4. Claims/Cancellations will review, revise, and implement an efficient process for journal and serial titles claims and cancellations on our local system vendor's, Innovative Interfaces Inc., new Millennium Silver release. Information Resources managers reported during our current needs assessment that many serial titles were inaccurate or that claiming cycles were not being effectively enforced. TSAP goal will be to find solutions to the various issues raised concerning this area of work.

5. Web Overhaul will work with the Guided User Interface Design Group, an appointed library-wide group charged to retool the library's website, to identify TSAP forms and materials that need to be incorporated into the new developing library web page. In addition this group will evaluate, plan, and develop virtual review shelves, including damaged materials, gifts, reference, and replacements, among others, and computer-based training applications for students and temporary employees. Our 2004 needs assessment also had several admonitions about finding information on our website, and TSAP needs to automate some of the simpler training processes that we use to train both students and temporary employees because of the increasing reliance on their work and the turnover that occurs on a yearly basis.

6. Accumulations will again this year review and revise the standing list of backlogs and accumulations that have not yet been cataloged. After the Accumulations team discusses the revised list with IR managers, temporary employees will be hired to process the next two to three categories of materials to provide access for our customers.

PLANNING PROCESS

Depending on the size of the projects identified for the year, TSAP members begin to organize the project team memberships and activities. In the library's team environment, TSAP is led by a standing

Leadership Team (Leadership) composed of the team leader, four work team leaders, a second representative from each work team, and the Materials Budget, Procurement, and Licensing librarian. This group is responsible for providing team-wide leadership, establishing team policies, and maintaining team-wide communications. As a leadership body, it also takes responsibility for writing the team charges for the projects created during the annual spring strategic planning retreat. For each of the projects outlined in the previous section, Leadership appoints a sponsor. It is the sponsor's responsibility to draft the charge, bring it back to Leadership for review, and ultimately hand off the charge to the project team appointees.

Each charge outlines the problem/purpose to be addressed, the context/background, parameters under which the team is working, the expected product or outcome, a general set of milestones or schedule of events, the available resources, the roles of appointees, expected time needed per week for each appointee, the necessary skills and abilities of the appointees, and the proposed membership of the team. These charges vary in length from two to six pages.

Leadership identifies and appoints TSAP staff to work on the projects during the fiscal year. The sponsor serves as liaison from the project teams back to Leadership. They are responsible for identifying and assisting in removing barriers to the team's work including communicating any financial support the team might need to complete its work. For instance, the Web Overhaul project team needed additional software to create pages for the new TSAP training website. An allocation was made to cover this need from TSAP's operating budget.

In some cases, a project is critical enough to influence an organizational change on a basic level for a prescribed amount of time. This was the case with the Electronic Resources project, which was identified during the retreat for critical need. To accommodate this, TSAP established a separate, temporary work team. Specific staff was charged with the responsibilities of implementing and documenting the processes necessary to support the use of our new subsystem, Innovative Interfaces Electronic Resources Management. Figure 6.2 reflects how TSAP reorganized.

This was implemented in July 2004 with an assessment to occur in December 2004 to determine whether this special team should be continued or disbanded. The Electronic Resources Team was reaf-

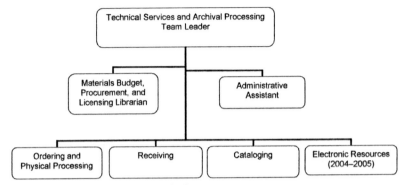

Figure 6.2. TSAP Organizational Chart, 2004

firmed in December to continue through June 2005, with another assessment to occur during the retreat for planning the 2005–2006 fiscal year.

INDIVIDUAL PERFORMANCE GOALS

Once appointees know their assigned project(s), they begin working (this generally happens within TSAP in the May–July time frame), and they are in a position to write their individual performance goals for the year. Aside from primary functional responsibilities and goals, each staff member will have at least one performance goal reflecting work and outcomes on his or her strategic plan projects. As staff develop their individual goals for the fiscal year, they build the peer review teams that will assist them in monitoring their progress toward their goal outputs and achievements. Some work teams within TSAP employ their whole work team as peer group reviewers for each member and include additional members if the work they have been assigned takes them outside the actual functional work of the work team.

On a quarterly basis the staff members write updates on their progress and meet with their peer review teams for input. At the end of each of these quarterly meetings, the individuals summarize the input from their peers and file a copy of the report. The team leader reviews each of the summaries and adds additional comments as necessary. For the team leader, it provides a method of keeping up with each individual's progress throughout the year, as well as tracking the progress for the team's special projects.

During the year staff become eligible for Career Progression and Merit (CP/M), the library's current method of compensating exceptional work by staff for the library. Merit increases are based on completed work with positive, effective outcomes for the library. Individual staff who wish to apply prepare a document outlining their accomplishments over the last year or two, emphasizing those accomplishments that have benefited the library directly and have measurable outcomes. After writing the document, the individual gives it to the peer review group, which reads, evaluates, and comments on the proposal. The individual takes these comments, updates the proposal, and forwards it to a library-wide peer review group, which does a final evaluation and determines whether a merit award is justified.

In this way, through project identification, functional work, individual developmental goals, and finally, library-wide evaluation of an individual's work, the merit system is linked back to measurable outcomes that positively benefit the library's strategic plan and the university plan as a whole.

TEAM REPORTING AND ASSESSMENT

Each individual staff's performance impacts the success of the team throughout the year. In addition to individual performance goals, performance measures and quality standards must be maintained at the team level. Many of these measurements are based on quantitative measurements of success, that is, processing of materials orders (100 percent of the time an order will be placed within twenty-four hours) or copy cataloging upon receipt (95 percent of materials will be received and copy cataloged within ten days of receipt).

To keep the entire team informed, each work team and TSAP cross-functional team reports to the team as a whole on a monthly basis, and TSAP reports to the library on a quarterly basis. TSAP work team and cross-functional team monthly reports serve as a check on progress for the current projects and allow for discussion of issues or barriers encountered with team members. These monthly reports also serve as the foundation for TSAP's report to the library during each quarter.

Quarterly, each library team reports on the status of its quality standards and also highlights one or two projects that were established at the beginning of the fiscal year. Open discussion follows the team presentations. In this way, staff and faculty across the library can be informed about and seek clarification on each team's progress for the year. The reports also serve as a platform to raise issues from the team's perspective on any barriers or concerns the team has uncovered since the last report. It is not necessary to wait for the next quarterly meeting, however. Any team can schedule an open dialogue session with the library when and if issues arise that necessitate exploration by the library as a whole.

Within TSAP, Leadership oversees the preparation of the library's quarterly reports. The responsibility for presentation of the content moves from one work team to the next throughout the year. Reports take the form of a PowerPoint presentation with an updated written report on the statuses of each quality standard.

In this way the planning comes full circle in the library for consideration and evaluation. The library is able to focus on those issues for the year that are key to its success. The library's success is in turn founded on each individual's developmental goals and achievements and the successes of its teams. It is in this way that the Technical Services and Archival Processing Team has become a more effective participant in the library's encompassing team structure at the University of Arizona Library.

APPENDIX: TSAP STRATEGIC PLANNING 2004–2005, QUESTIONS FOR NEEDS ASSESSMENT PLANNING, FEBRUARY 2004

1. Below are listed TSAP's current processes. Based on your experience over the last few years, could you answer the following questions:
   a. What do we need to change or add to these processes to help your team meet its objectives?
   b. What are your expectations from TSAP concerning these processes?
   c. Is there anything here that you can identify that we can stop doing and still meet your expectations for these processes?

Processes

> Ordering: Place orders requiring preorder searching; creation of order in SABIO/Collection Manager; distribution of orders; loading and processing of order records; claiming; tracking renewals and vendor reports; processing Reserve rush requests; order records maintenance; and general order problem solving.
>
> Receiving: Receive monographic and serial titles; copy catalog materials, including videos; process items without copy to Frontlog; check in periodicals; claiming; tracking vendor reports on serial titles that are delayed; processing Reserve and credit card requests; loading and processing record files from books and document vendors; processing duplicate returns; invoice processing; and general receiving problem solving and database maintenance.
>
> Cataloging & Electronic Resources: Catalog scores, maps, and other special materials; manage TechPro original cataloging shipments; copy catalog Frontlogs from Main and Team Y [Spec Coll]; process rare and special materials resident in Special Collections Library; withdraw materials; and SABIO catalog database maintenance.
>
> E-journal related responsibilities include ordering, cataloging, and linking new and revised full-text materials; licensing full-text materials; and maintaining Serials Solutions and Electronic Resource Management system databases.
>
> Physical Processing: Prepare all materials entering the library for shelving, for example, tattle taping, labeling, pam binding; manage bindery shipments to and from our binder; and repairs.

2. Considering your current and projected team's projects, is there anything that you think TSAP can or should do to assist?
3. Have you ever asked for TSAP assistance in the past? Briefly describe the request and what you thought about the response.
4. If you could change one thing about TSAP, what would it be?

NOTES

1. "The University of Arizona Library Mission, Goals, & Strategies," May 4, 2004. http://dizzy.library.arizona.edu/library/teams/slrp/statements/mission.html (accessed March 24, 2005).

2. "The University of Arizona Library Mission, Goals, & Strategies."

3. The University of Arizona Technical and Archival Processing Team, "TSAP Vision-Mission Statements for 2005/2006." www.library.arizona.edu/library/teams/tsap/TSTvision_mission.htm (accessed March 24, 2005).

4. The University of Arizona Library Mission, Goals, & Strategies."

5. The University of Arizona Technical Services and Archival Processing Team, "Strategic Framework Plan For 2004/2005," last updated February 10, 2005. www.library.arizona.edu/library/teams/tsap/StrategicPlan0405.htm (accessed March 24, 2005).

Chapter 7

Team Training for Technical Services: Revisiting the Concept after Ten Years

Paul Orkiszewski, Megan Johnson,
and Eleanor I. Cook

The Appalachian State University Libraries have operated in a team envi-ronment since 1995, and there has been little training done on the concept since teams were initially established. In the ten years since implementa-tion, a number of changes have occurred. A new integrated library system has been installed, staff and faculty members have left or retired, new posi-tions have been created, some team structures have been tweaked, and the library planned for and moved into a new building in May 2005. To revi-talize and strengthen interest in the team structure and to orient personnel who never received team training in the first place, the library's Personnel Development Committee planned for training with an outside facilitator to take place in the fall of 2004.

To determine the effectiveness of this training, technical services team members completed an anonymous survey before training to establish a baseline and then completed a second survey afterward to determine the re-sults of the training. This chapter is a reflection of what worked, what did not, and other insights on staff perceptions of working in team environ-ments.

The Carol Grotnes Belk Library at Appalachian State University has operated with a team structure since 1995. In 1992, when the current university librarian arrived, she brought with her new ideas about how the library should be managed. Prior to this time, Belk Library had been organized in a standard hierarchical mode. After a lengthy process of study and then implementation, the library began to fully

121

operate in teams, which it still does to this day. For further background on this shift and its impact on the technical services operation during the time of implementation, see Eleanor Cook and Pat Farthing, "A Technical Services Perspective of Implementing an Organizational Review While Simultaneously Installing an Integrated Library System."

How has the team structure fared since 1995? Between 1994 and 1995, the shift to teams was stressful but also brought needed changes. Department heads as such were eliminated and were replaced by coordinators. The number of coordinators was reduced, allowing some faculty to return to the front lines of service. The coordinator role, while not so different from that of department head in some ways, was and is less directive in spirit and more focused on coaching and supporting, allowing team members more say in the development of new procedures and service initiatives. The number of assistant directors went from two to one, and the remaining individual became associate director. Divisiveness between technical and public services areas lessened as faculty and staff took on more diverse responsibilities and got the chance to see how "the other half" lived. Collection development activities were more closely defined and strengthened with the establishment of a team of subject specialists. Reference and Instruction, at first two separate teams that later merged back into one team, gained insights from including some of their technical services colleagues in their activities. A new team, Information Organization, was developed to address emerging technologies such as the World Wide Web and online databases. (This team has evolved into a simple committee.) A Systems and Automation Team was formalized to acknowledge the ever increasingly important role that computer support was gaining in the library. Finally, Circulation, Interlibrary Loan, and several other format-based public service points were combined to become the Access Team. The special area collections—the Music Library, the Appalachian Collection, and the Instructional Materials Center (IMC) remained intact as special entities, although it took the IMC a couple of years to regain that status after being initially decentralized. In 1996, as distance education became an important part of the university's focus, a Distance Education Team was formed.

For the technical services realm, the move to teams had several major impacts. Prior to reorganization, separate departments all reporting to an associate university librarian (AUL) for technical services existed for the functions of acquisitions, cataloging, serials, and collection management. After reorganization, a new combined team named Materials Processing brought acquisitions, cataloging, and serials together into one entity. For better or worse, the new name brought a new identity and cast out any connotations associated with the old departments. Initially there was one coordinator and an assistant coordinator. In 2000, with the impending retirement of the coordinator, the team took it upon themselves to review the team's structure. After three sessions with a campus facilitator, a report was completed and the recommendation accepted that the lead functional specialists in acquisitions, cataloging, and serials all needed to be considered coordinators. The team however, continued to exist as a single entity organizationally. This is the way the team has operated ever since. In practice, acquisitions, cataloging, and serials think of themselves as specialized units operating within the Materials Processing Team.

In October 2004, the cataloging coordinator left to accept a position at another university. The acquisitions coordinator is currently also serving as the acting cataloging coordinator until a decision is reached whether or not to replace the cataloging coordinator position as it is or with different duties.

What has really changed over the years? Materials Processing staff and faculty, once separated into smaller departments who, though needing to constantly work closely together, bickered with each other over process, turf, resources, and influence, now are all one big happy family. Is this really true? For the most part, yes, it is! While specialized units for different functions still exist, crossover and cross-training are easier to achieve, and any time a given unit has a special need, the others are quick to come to their aid if need be.

TEAM TRAINING

By 2004, nine years after the implementation of the team structure, there was a general sense within the library that we needed a refresher course in team management. The library was moving into a new building, and it was an important time to build spirit and improve communication. Faculty and staff understanding of the purpose and functioning of teams varied from person to person and team to team. In large part, this ambiguity was caused by turnover of personnel. Eight out of thirteen team coordinators were new to the library after numerous retirements during the 1990s. Within Materials Processing, most of the staff had experienced the original reorganization, but four out of six faculty librarians employed in fall 2005 had not. To reinvigorate and improve the collective understanding of team management, the library's Personnel Development Committee planned a team-training session with an outside facilitator, who conducted the workshop in November 2004. The authors decided to do a brief anonymous survey before and after the workshops, to determine technical services staff members' perceptions (see the appendix). To prepare the survey, we consulted with the director of Institutional Research Assessment and Planning (IRAP) at Appalachian State University, and with the facilitator who was preparing for the team training. The IRAP director advised us to remove "neutral" answers on our questions that ranged from "strongly agree" to "strongly disagree." The facilitator provided insight into the directions she would be taking. For example, the question "What are your team's shared values?" was directly related to a segment of the training.

SURVEY RESULTS

The results of both surveys indicated that most staff members perceived the team environment favorably, and most (twelve out of fifteen) believed training helps people operate better on teams. The questions were designed to see if the training changed staff perceptions. In answer to the question about the team's shared values, for example, in the first round of responses, staff used the term "accuracy" or a variation on "speed" in shared values, but after training the word "respect" appeared in two-thirds of the responses.

The response to the query "Training helps people operate better on a team" with four choices ranging from "strongly agree" to "strongly disagree" was revealing. In both the before and after surveys, three respondents out of fifteen (quite likely the same three people) disagreed with the statement. This does not necessarily reflect on the quality of the training or its usefulness for the team. In any group, there will be disagreement about the usefulness of any activity, including staff development training, which may, to some, seem a nebulous and unnecessary distraction from the work at hand.

In the final question, which is a solicitation for "Any other comments?" several staff members expressed frustration with the amount of team training. Some agreed with one statement that "it is ridiculous to wait ten years between training sessions." Others cautioned against over-training, however. For example, "the law of diminishing returns applies; some is good but too much isn't worth it."

In the follow-up survey, only two staff members had additional comments, and one was very positive, saying it was "superior to anything we did in the past," but the second was more qualified, saying it would be valuable only if there was follow-through. When asked if they found the surveys helpful, one staff member said he or she was glad the survey was anonymous because "it allows people to say what they really feel . . . maybe it will help people sort out where they stand."

In general, people were slightly more positive in their survey responses after training than before, but the survey did not indicate that there was a measurable difference in staff perceptions.

The team-training workshop was held offsite at the university's conference center and lasted one day. Library personnel worked with their usual teams through a series of exercises designed to build teams and strengthen communication. In most of the exercises, individuals responded to questions on handouts, responses were transcribed to large tear sheets, and the groups discussed the meanings and implications of the topics and responses. Some of the exercises resulted in documents the teams could use for further development. For example, the first exercise led the teams through the process of defining consensual values and behaviors (Table 7.1). These were created through individual brainstorming, sharing ideas with the group, and establishing consensus through debating and voting. The team values and behaviors were purposely broad, and most of the behaviors, such as treating others as you would like to be treated, being flexible, or maintaining a sense of humor, are applicable to any organization or social group. As would be expected in a team environment, the team chose values that stress interpersonal relations such as respect, cooperation, and communication.

The second exercise was designed to help team members and leaders reach consensus on roles. The team looked at a list of

Table 7.1. Shared Team Values and Behaviors

Team Value	Behaviors
Respect	• Say "good morning." • Respect the ideas and feelings of others. • Golden rule: Treat others as you would like to be treated.
Cooperation	• Concentrate on what we can do, not what we can't do. • Be willing to accept alternatives. • Focus on team goals. • Be flexible in day-to-day assignments. • Trust the work of others.
Responsibility	• Meet deadlines, goals, and service standards. • Step in when needed. • Be consistent.
Communication	• Have a shared understanding of standards. • Read e-mails and listen in meetings. • Share news and participate in meetings.
Fun	• Maintain perspective and sense of humor.

responsibilities, and individuals designated each responsibility as being either for the team member, for the team leader, or shared. Table 7.2 shows the tally of how responsibilities were distributed. In all but one case, the majority thought that responsibilities are shared between team members and leaders, which points to an

Table 7.2. Roles and Responsibilities of Team Members and Leaders

Responsibility	Members	Leaders	Shared
Setting goals	0	1	13
Ensure quality of meetings	0	2	12
Assign, direct individual work	0	9	5
Resolve differences and conflict	0	1	13
Describe vision and direction for team	0	0	14
Develop individuals	2	1	11
Mentor and coach	1	3	10
Distribute information	0	3	11
Coordinate multiple activities	0	5	9
Build trust and respect	0	1	13
Develop policies and procedures	0	1	13
Represent team to other teams	0	6	8
Ensure team goals are met	0	0	14

Note: Numbers represent people who thought responsibilities belonged to team members or team leaders, or were shared.

Table 7.3. Features of Good and Poor Communication

Good Communication	Poor Communication
Cross-membership in teams	Lack of contact
Mutual respect	Disrespect
Professionalism at all levels	Unjust criticism
Willingness to participate	Gossip
Understanding of roles	Lack of understanding
Empathy	Paranoia
Cooperation	Grudges
Sharing	Power-mongering
	Judging

existing sense of team unity and an understanding of team management.

One of the last exercises focused on factors contributing to good or poor communication. Again, the method was to move from individual ideas through sharing and discussion to reach consensus. Table 7.3 shows the team's ideas of features of good and poor communication. Some of these were inspired by particular events in the team's past and may have caused some tension by bringing up past difficulties. However, the exercise helped the team to think about the importance of communication within the group and how to improve communication both individually and as a team.

Other exercises addressed communication and relationships between teams, how to assess communication within the teams, and the types of conflict the team experiences and how they address them. The final exercise resulted in five goals for the Materials Processing Team:

1. Keep having fun and a sense of humor through upcoming changes and the library move.
2. Communicate directly when there are issues.
3. Be willing to accept changes and diverse personalities.
4. Team members share the workload and are treated equally.
5. Put into effect all positive outcomes of this workshop to form a stronger team, and be assured that the library administration acknowledges and values our opinions regarding the needs of our team.

Materials Processing Team members cooperated and participated in the exercises, and the day-long event went well. Many staff members, however, thought it had not been a valuable use of their time, especially for those who remembered the original training in 1995. One point that came up repeatedly during the day was that communication and cooperation within the team seemed to be working well, but communication and cooperation across teams was a continuing problem that was not addressed in the workshop. At the end of the day, library coordinators met separately to discuss the workshop and planned how to move forward.

The facilitator returned in March 2005 for follow-up meetings with selected library teams, Materials Processing being one of them. Meetings with the remaining teams were held in fall 2005. In the interim, another outside consultant was brought in to address how to fill the vacant coordinator position in Cataloging and to analyze workflow within the entire Materials Processing operation. Understandably, the team was beginning to experience "consultant fatigue." All staff were feeling pressure to be at their desks working on backlogs of uncataloged materials or on projects and preparing for the library's move rather than discussing the team structure. One staff member commented, "After you're done talking today, are we going to be finally fixed?" However, to their credit, most team members started with an open attitude and were willing to engage in the process.

The purpose of the second session with the team-training facilitator was to follow up on the goals the team had assigned themselves at the first session and to furnish the team with strategies for dealing with communication issues, especially with other library teams.

In the discussion, it became apparent that there is a natural tension in the team model. While there are advantages to making decisions collaboratively, it is sometimes less stressful to just be clearly told what needs to be done. The shift of responsibility for action from a "supervisor" to "the team" sometimes contributes to poor communication and lack of accountability, not only internally, but also in dealing with other teams.

Another thing that became very apparent was the ambiguity of the coordinator role causing confusion not only in Materials Processing, but also across the library. Although the team model was implemented ten years ago, the role of the coordinator has never been clearly defined, and it varies somewhat from team to team. As one team member said, "As many of us as are sitting at this table, that is how many opinions there are about what the role of the coordinator is." The facilitator advised the Materials Processing Team to define the role of the coordinator now, for themselves, before it is decided for them from outside the team.

The tools and strategies the team received to improve communication included tips on running more efficient meetings, guidelines on how to communicate better, how to better communicate their value to other teams in the library, and how to better demonstrate the costs and benefits of the service the Materials Processing Team provides to the library as a whole.

Has this training helped? One team member commented afterward, "Yes, it was time well spent. If people are willing to grow, it will help them." Another person observed that "It's mostly just talk. But if people learned even one thing, like how to run a meeting better, we will all be better off."

ACKNOWLEDGMENTS

The authors thank the Materials Processing Team, the Personnel Development Committee of Appalachian State University Library, and Dr. Shelia Creth for the time and energy spent on this process so that we were able to complete this chapter.

APPENDIX: SURVEY

This anonymous survey will be conducted two times—once before the training, and once immediately following the initial session. The goal is to determine what aspect(s) of the training was helpful, and what technical services staff perceptions of working in a team are.

The purpose of conducting this survey is to publish a brief case study in an upcoming Scarecrow Press book on Teams in Technical Services.

Thank you for your input, Eleanor Cook, Paul Orkiszewski, Megan Johnson.

1. Did you work at Belk Library when the original team structure was instituted?   Yes ☐ No ☐

Did you go through team training?   Yes ☐ No ☐
Did you find the training helpful?   Yes ☐ No ☐
Comments? _____

2. My group operates as a team:
   ☐ Strongly agree
   ☐ Agree
   ☐ Disagree
   ☐ Strongly disagree

3. What are your team's shared values?
   _____

4. What are some characteristics of effective teams?
   _____

5. How is your team accountable for supporting the library's goals?
   _____

6. My team manages conflict well:
   ☐ Strongly agree
   ☐ Agree
   ☐ Disagree
   ☐ Strongly disagree

7. Training helps people operate better on a team:
   ☐ Strongly agree
   ☐ Agree
   ☐ Disagree
   ☐ Strongly disagree

8. Any other comments:
   _____

BIBLIOGRAPHY

Caudron, Shari. "Keeping Team Conflict Alive." *Training and Development* 52, no. 9 (1998): 48–52.

Cook, Eleanor I., and Pat Farthing. "A Technical Services Perspective of Implementing an Organizational Review While Simultaneously Installing an Integrated Library System." *Library Acquisitions: Practice and Theory* 19, no. 4 (Winter 1995): 445–461.

Hackett, Thomas J. "Giving Teams a Tune-up." *HR Focus* 74, no. 11 (November 1997): 11.

Hultman, Kenneth E. "The Ten Commandments of Team Leadership." *Training and Development* 52, no. 2 (February 1998): 12.

Katzenbach, Jon R., and Douglas K. Smith. "The Discipline of Teams." *Harvard Business Review* 71, no. 2 (March/April 1993): 111–120.

Part 3

REEVALUATION OF
THE TEAM STRUCTURE

Chapter 8

Transitioning from Self-Directed Teams to a Traditional Work Unit

Robert Alan

A growing body of management literature suggests that self-directed work teams may be more productive at a lower cost than traditional hierarchical organizational models. The self-directed work team model suggests that teams bring together complementary skills and experience that exceed those of any individual on a team. This combination of skill sets enables teams to respond as a whole with more innovative solutions to problems, higher productivity, and improved customer service. However, for self-directed work teams to be successful, team members need to be committed to the new organizational model and develop management and communications skills sufficient to support team and organizational goals.

Although self-directed work teams are considered to be a departure from traditional management philosophy, teams have also demonstrated their value in libraries. However, there are conditions when self-directed work teams may not be effective and require changes to the model to ensure successful outcomes. Evaluation of unsuccessful teams may result in the need to transition back to more traditional supervised work units.

A self-directed work team has been defined as a group of employees who have day-to-day authority for managing themselves and the work they do with a minimum of direct supervision.[1] The benefits of teams and team building have been documented in management literature and, to a lesser extent, library literature. While most conclusions are based on case studies, there is a growing body of empirical research that suggests that self-directed work teams can be more productive than traditional hierarchical organizational models.

There is also evidence that self-directed work teams should be applied only in work contexts that are deemed advantageous for their use.[2] There are factors that can limit the effectiveness of self-directed work teams. Such factors as team leadership, accountability, and organizational culture can directly affect the level of success achieved by teams.

Katzenbach and Smith indicate that one of the advantages of team models is that teams have much more fun than traditional hierarchical work units.[3] However, that may not be the case when there are significant barriers that affect the development and maintenance of a positive work environment.

The purpose of this chapter is to explore the reasons why two of three self-directed work teams in the Penn State Libraries Serials Department did not achieve a high level of success. The teams' inability to overcome both internal and external barriers to team development led to the need to reassess the team structure and make alterations to improve the quantity and quality of work completed, customer service, and the quality of work life within the department.

BACKGROUND

In 1994, the Penn State Libraries Acquisitions Services Department implemented self-directed work teams. At that time, serial acquisition functions (ordering, check-in, claiming, and invoice payment) were incorporated with monographic acquisition functions in Acquisitions Services and serials cataloging within the Cataloging Services Department.

The reorganization to self-directed work teams was in response to a campus initiative that directed all units within the university to reduce nonstrategic program spending to make additional funding available to better support strategic initiatives.[4] The university considered the collections budget strategic to the mission, and therefore, operations budgets were targeted for reduction.

Prior to reorganizing into self-directed work teams, Acquisitions Services' organization was extremely hierarchical with six levels of management.[5] Management included a department head, four librarians who served as section heads, two coordinators, and four staff supervisors. Staff members were assigned to one of five functional areas: approval plans, ordering, invoice/claims, monographic receiving, and continuations. The Continuing Order Team was responsible for serials ordering, receiving, claiming, and invoice processing.[6]

The model was both costly and inefficient due to the number of librarians and supervisors and levels in the decision-making hierarchy. Michie and West describe staff involvement in decision making as being along a continuum:[7]

- Only management makes decisions and is completely responsible.
- Management makes decisions but asks for staff input.
- Decisions are made jointly.
- Staff make decisions but ask for management input.
- Only staff make decisions and are completely responsible for them.

Current staff members who were members of Acquisitions Services in 1994 reported that the pre-1994 model did not support staff involvement in decision making. Prior to the reorganization, decision making was made primarily by management with limited staff input. Proponents of teams think that by altering the structure of an organization to reduce the management hierarchy and empowering staff to participate in decision making, employee satisfaction and output will increase.[8]

Following the 1994 reorganization to self-directed work teams, Acquisitions Services had only one librarian position that served as department head. In self-directed work teams, team members were expected to manage daily operations, establish and monitor team performance, train and mentor new teammates, and manage many personnel functions within the team that were formerly the responsibility of the supervisor.[9] The role of the department head changed to one of team advisor, developing the self-managing skills of each team through coaching, training, and counseling.

FORMATION OF THE SERIALS DEPARTMENT

The reorganization into self-directed work teams had mixed results for the Acquisitions Services Continuing Order Team. From 1994 to 1999 there was the perception within the Penn State Libraries that serials were not being well managed. The reorganization left only one librarian within Acquisitions Services who served as department head. The department head was expected to serve as an advocate for all monographic and serial acquisition issues and provide managerial oversight of the self-directed work teams.

In response to the concerns, a task force was formed in 1999 and charged to

- Review the serial ordering, receipt, and cataloging process and identify problem areas and areas for creating more efficient processes
- Recommend steps to maximize efficiencies of serials processing
- Recommend staffing and organizational structures that would lead to more efficient serials management

A survey confirmed that the customers did not have confidence that serial acquisition functions were being well managed. Problems identified by customers included the full range of serials fulfillment and access issues. Claiming, lapsed serial subscriptions, and invoice processing were identified as being particularly problematic.

The task force recommended creating a separate serials department that would be responsible for all functional areas of serials management, including serials cataloging. The mission of the newly formed Serials Department was to acquire, manage, and provide access to serial resources in all formats in an accurate, timely manner while maintaining a high level of customer service.

SERIALS DEPARTMENT ORGANIZATION (2000–2004)

The Serials Department was originally organized into three self-directed work teams under a new department head position (Figure 8.1). The original Acquisitions Services Continuing Order Team was split into the Receiving Team and Ordering and Invoicing Team. The Serials Cataloging Team transferred from Cataloging Services as the third team in the new department.

Team responsibilities included the following:

- The Receiving Team (five full-time and one part-time staff) was responsible for all serials receiving functions. These included check-in, first claims, and processing of serials and periodicals for most Penn State locations. The Receiving Team also managed processing of materials received on standing orders (e.g., monographic series), blanket orders, and memberships.

- The Ordering and Invoicing Team (three full-time staff) was responsible for managing ordering, payment, and claiming for subscriptions, standing orders, blanket orders, memberships, and replacement orders. The team also managed serial gifts and exchanges.
- The Serials Cataloging Team (three full-time staff) was responsible for serials cataloging and maintenance for most Penn State campus locations. This team's workloads were greatly impacted by the rapid growth in electronic resources prior to the format change impacting the other two teams.

The Serials Department's three self-directed work teams were initially expected to handle internal job assignments, prioritize and manage workloads, develop and document procedures, and take action on problems.

The new department head position would provide oversight to the teams in the same sense as the Acquisitions Services department head, serving as team advisor but also as the department's supervisor. In addition, the department head would provide library-wide leadership for print serials and electronic resources management and access issues.

The task force recommended that electronic resources management be incorporated within the new Serials Department. Therefore, the department needed to begin the process of eventually transitioning from a department that managed primarily print to a department that would soon be responsible for managing both print and electronic resources.

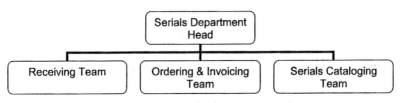

Figure 8.1.   Serials Department Organization, 2000–2004

The task force recommended hiring a librarian serials cataloger to serve as liaison to the Serials Cataloging Team. However, that position was not created due to budgetary constraints.

The newly formed Serials Department began operations in January 2000, and a permanent department head was appointed in September 2000.

TEAM DEVELOPMENT

The recommendation to form a new department that focused on serials was based on the need to improve overall production and customer service. The goal of bringing together the serial acquisition and cataloging functions into a single department was to improve communication and streamline serial acquisition and cataloging processes. However, it quickly became apparent that the formation of a separate Serials Department alone would not necessarily result in improved performance.

The transition to a new department was not an easy one for many staff. While all staff attended training sessions presented by Penn State's Human Resources Development Center on topics such as team building, communications, and conflict management, not all staff members responded in a positive manner to the sessions.

While all staff members clearly supported the reorganization that led to the formation of the Serials Department, some staff expressed unhappiness with the team structure and work climate.

ASSESSMENT OF TEAM STRUCTURE (2001–2003)

The assessment of the team structure began very soon after the arrival of the permanent department head. Individual staff interviews combined with weekly team meetings, and observation provided important insight into the current organizational culture. One of the primary goals of these sessions was not only to get to know individual staff members but also to build a level of trust between staff, teams, and the department head. Standard performance indicators such as quantity and quality of work completed were included in the assessment. It was concluded that at the very least incremental changes would need to be made to the current team structure over time to address problems and improve performance. There were several factors that contributed to this conclusion.

STAGES OF TEAM DEVELOPMENT

Development of successful self-directed work teams is an evolutionary process that can be both time consuming and frustrating. The implementation of a new integrated library management system combined with the need to immediately restore customer confidence in serials management required that action be taken in the near term.

Management literature offers different views of how successful teams should be developed. While many offer recipes for success, all approaches address, in some form, the planning, implementation, and assessment process. However, since the Serials Department's self-directed work teams were put in place at the time of the reorganization, a postreorganization assessment was required.

The goal was to identify factors that served as barriers to team development. From the outset, it was apparent that the department's three teams operated at different levels.

Wellins, Byham, and Wilson describe four stages of team development:[10]

- Stage one is characterized by tentative communications within the team, mixed team involvement in decision making, and general feeling of confusion, ambivalence, and annoyance in decision making.
- During stage two routines emerge and are standardized. For example, teams will incorporate daily team huddles or develop regular routines for monitoring workloads.
- By stage three team members have become more comfortable in the team environment, and the team as a whole is able to focus on processes and team goals.
- Stage four, the most advanced stage, reflects a team that now embraces diversity, respects different skills sets and honest differences of opinion, and is proactive. However, at stage four, the team may consider team goals more important than broader organizational goals.

They suggest several indicators of the stages of development:[11]

- Members are commited to the team structure and organization.
- Trust within the team leads to open communication and respect.
- Team has a clear vision of its purpose but is also flexible and able to adapt to change.
- All team members are involved in the management and decision-making process.
- Team processes are a regular part of the workplace environment.

When the criteria were applied to the newly formed Serials Department, it was clear that the Receiving and the Ordering and Invoicing Teams had reached only stage two. Both of these teams had difficulty agreeing within and across teams on workflows, procedures, and priorities. Individual goals often took precedence over team or organizational goals. Many decisions were based on personal preferences rather than the objective application of sound business and library practices. The Receiving and Ordering and Invoicing Teams required continuous intervention from the department head to address individual and team performance issues.

The Serials Cataloging Team had probably reached stage three or at times stage four. Customer feedback indicated a very high level of satisfaction in service provided by the team. Team members were comfortable and supportive of each other and maintained a positive work climate based on mutual respect for each individual's skill levels and contributions to their team and department.

LACK OF COMMITMENT TO TEAM STRUCTURE

There was reluctance on the part of many Serials Department staff toward self-directed work teams. This reluctance or indifference to the team structure was an important factor. Katzenbach and Smith state that there are several major factors that can inhibit team development:[12]

- Insufficient commitment to team performance
- Weak sense of direction within the team

- Critical skill gaps
- Indifference to the team structure

Within the Serials Department there was a lack of conviction by individuals that the current team structure was better than alternative approaches. Some staff seemed uncomfortable and therefore unhappy working on a self-directed work team. This may have been due to personal preferences based on individual capabilities and interests.

Successful self-management depends on effective coordination and team spirit.[13] When staff are not committed to the team structure, it is difficult to build a high level of team spirit. It is also difficult to bring new staff into the organization. When there was team member turnover, considerable time was lost orienting new team members to technical requirements and the way that the team should work together. A lack of continuity resulted in team performance problems due to lost time and the expectation that new team members would be trained within the team. If training was inadequate, performance problems for individuals and teams would continue. Newer staff members often had difficulty gaining all the knowledge they needed to be successful in their positions.

TASK VERSUS CONTEXTUAL PERFORMANCE

An important distinction needed to be made between task performance and contextual performance. Task performance relates to the core tasks assigned to an individual or team, while contextual performance refers to less measurable but equally important activities outside the core tasks.[14] Examples of contextual activities incorporated within the structure of a self-directed work team would be rotating administrator activities, team representatives on committees, and mentoring or counseling of other team members. It is important to note that poor contextual performance may, and often will, have a direct impact on task performance. Many of the tasks associated with contextual performance are key elements in the team structure.

In terms of the Serials Department, staff on all teams demonstrated a very strong work ethic and wanted to do the best job possible. Skill levels for core tasks varied based on the level of training and feedback, as well as ability to accept constructive feedback.

While it was expected that problems with task performance were correctible if training was upgraded, contextual performance was more difficult to address. In part this was due to a lack of commitment to the team structure by some staff. While all three teams wanted to continue to be empowered to manage core tasks, there was a consensus that at least some of the self-management aspects of the team structure were too time consuming and should now become the responsibility of the department head.

LEADERSHIP DILEMMA

Team leadership versus department leadership proved to be an important factor that contributed to the decision to change the structure of the self-directed work teams. The role for the department head as supervisor/manager was an important consideration for the Serials Department's self-directed work teams. Manz and Sims describe leadership of self-directed work teams as being a paradox.[15] How does one manage and supervise self-directed work teams that are expected to manage themselves? The role of the department head in a team environment is to counsel, facilitate, and intervene only when issues (whether personal or business related) cannot be successfully resolved within the team. However, the department head is also ultimately held accountable for the team's and department's performance.

Over time the more dominant, long-term team members took on the role of supervisors, maintaining or attempting to maintain the team's authority system. Dominant members of teams would often control, not lead, others based on stronger personality traits rather than demonstrated management or job skills. Cliques formed led by one of the dominant team members. These cliques within and across teams eventually replicated to some degree a system of hierarchy within the teams, with dominant long-term, full-time staff on top, and staff less interested in participating in team politics plus newer and part-time staff on the bottom.

All too often the chronic complainers within the Serials Department were the ones who were most vocal and made their opinions known. And these same individuals did not appear to have the skills required to effectively separate personal from work-related issues. This was unfortunate, as these individuals tended to sway the opinions of those who were either intimidated or indifferent to the team and department. The more committed but less vocal staff members tended to keep their opinions to themselves and were excluded from the self-management process.

The dominant personalities who attempted to fill leadership roles on their teams could not accept receiving any type of negative feedback from teammates or other teams. Their approach was that the best defense was a good offense, as they would routinely attempt to move all blame from themselves to teammates or other teams. Other staff members were all too often bullied into taking the blame for the actions of others.

BULLYING

Rayner points out that it is difficult to define a bully, but a more straightforward approach would suggest simply that bullies "provide behaviors to which targets react negatively."[16] Within the Serials Department these behaviors took the form of personal attacks on staff members or entire teams. Examples of behaviors included gossiping and confrontations in meetings. The ongoing behavioral problems grew into performance problems that required the immediate intervention of the department head.

As a self-directed work team, unless the team determines how it will handle specific types of difficult situations, conflict management can result in ongoing problems that are difficult to quickly resolve. It is important during the formative stages that each team agree to norms, accountability, and conflict resolution procedures. While the staff had received training in conflict resolution, the gap in team leadership that dominant team members attempted to fill resulted in problems with bullying and accountability.

When one person is responsible as a supervisor for the performance of a unit, there is a clear understanding of accountability. To overcome some of the limitations of the team structure, the department head assumed more responsibility for management of the teams. While the teams continued to manage daily operations, all personnel issues were managed by the department head.

ABILITY TO ADAPT TO CHANGE

The newly formed Serials Department was expected to effectively manage significant organizational, environmental, and technological changes within a relatively limited time frame. An organization will experience planned and unplanned changes.[17] Planned changes included the formation of a new department and the restructuring of the teams, temporary relocation during a large library renovation and expansion project, and implementation of a new integrated library management system. Examples of unplanned changes included staffing changes, new unexpected workloads, and system implementation problems.

Studies indicate that there is a strong relationship between an organization's structure and culture. Unless the effort is made to adapt the organizational culture to complement structural change, the change will not be successful.[18] The change in the organizational structure did not coincide with the organizational culture leading to a breakdown in communications and maintenance of a positive work environment.

TRANSITION TO A SUPERVISED WORK UNIT (2003–2004)

Rationale for Organizational Change

The decision to move from self-directed work teams to a supervised work unit was not a group decision but a recommendation made by the department head after careful consideration of the relationship between team structure, organizational culture, and performance. Since alterations had already been made to the team structure in terms of leadership responsibility within teams, the transition to a supervised work unit was presented as the next logical step in altering the organization to improve the work environment and customer service. The department needed to quickly regain customer confidence and be better positioned to respond to new workloads associated with electronic resources management.

Organizational Culture and Climate Issues

The culture within an organization can be an asset or a liability. It had become apparent that splitting serial receiving and ordering and payment functions into two teams (Receiving and Ordering and Invoicing) had created boundaries that proved to be detrimental to the invoice payment and claiming processes that directly impacted management of the serials collection budgets. Effective serials management requires cooperation, communication, and a clear understanding of how all tasks and routines fit into the serials processing chain. But the Serials Department's organizational culture did not promote understanding, joint decision making, and effective communication. Therefore, it was concluded that the current organizational structure did not fit the needs of the Serials Department.

Staff Supervision and Management

The ability of self-directed work teams to internally manage diverse groups of personalities was questioned. The dominance of some staff over others did not promote a positive work environment and required intervention on the part of the department head. The Receiving and Ordering and Invoicing Teams had difficulty being held accountable for their performance problems.

Staff Skills and Knowledge Levels

There was a continuing need to upgrade staff skills and knowledge related to both task and contextual performance. In the self-directed work team structure, most training was managed within the teams. However, training was uneven, and as previously noted, newer staff did not have access to all information needed to be highly successful in their positions. There was an immediate need to upgrade training and documentation within the department.

PLANNING FOR THE TRANSITION

The first step in the planning process was to convene weekly department meetings chaired by the department head that focused only on serial processing issues. All other business was addressed in monthly department meetings. Weekly individual team meetings were soon discontinued, although the department head was available to meet with staff or teams.

Ground rules were established that required all attendees to respect everyone's opinions. Discussion based on personal bias was not permitted. Agenda setting and minute preparation were rotated among all staff.

The initial series of meetings was difficult as stronger personalities continued to attempt to dominate discussions. However, a supportive environment was eventually established, and the department meetings in part replaced the team support structure. As staff became more secure, they came to realize the need to be accountable for job performance.

The initial goal of the meetings was to move all operational decisions from the team level to the department level. Most operational decisions impact the work of all teams. Therefore, most decisions required input from each team, and all decisions needed to be more effectively communicated within the department.

Task Analysis

An important part of the planning process was completion of a task analysis by each team. A variation of activity-based costing was used to assign all tasks to broad categories and then subcategories.[19] Activity-based costing uses observation and interviews as the basis for determining the categories and subcategories of tasks as well as time assigned to each subcategory.[20] The only tasks for which time studies were conducted were basic core tasks such as check-in. All other tasks were assigned reasonable time estimates based on the experience of individuals assigned those tasks. Lower priority tasks not completed on a regular basis were still listed with time estimates.

Each team presented their findings at one of the weekly department meetings. Discussions followed that shed light on the way each team prioritized workloads. For example, the Receiving Team prided itself on checking in all periodical receipts within forty-eight hours of receipt in the department. This followed a lengthy period of time of significant check-in backlogs during the implementation of the new integrated library management system. The elimination of the backlogs was a great source of pride for the Receiving Team. However, the Ordering and Invoicing Team pointed out that first claims (formerly the responsibility of the Receiving Team) was an area that was not being adequately addressed. New procedures and reassignment of tasks followed that eventually improved claiming while maintaining timely receipt of serials. Staff quickly understood that cooperation across teams led to process improvements and job enrichment.

The task analysis took approximately three months to complete. Once it was completed, the department had a much better understanding of tasks assigned to each team and across teams. While teams continued to claim ownership of tasks, all tasks were now considered to be part of the overall serials-processing chain. It was important for staff at all levels to fully understand and appreciate the impact of their actions. If they did not do a good job, someone else may not be able to complete his or her job.

ADDRESSING STAFF CONCERNS

The most significant outcome of the task analysis was the recommendation that the Receiving and Ordering and Invoicing Teams eventually be rejoined into a single team or unit. While progress had been made in addressing serials management issues both within and across teams, boundaries remained based on personal differences that needed to be removed.

There was concern that by simply merging two teams into a larger team, there would be problems with self-management given the past history of both teams. Proponents of self-directed work teams also caution that larger teams can be problematic.[21] If a team is too large, subgroups or cliques may emerge that will be detrimental to team performance. However, the value of merging the Receiving and Ordering and Invoicing Teams into a single team outweighed concerns about the size of the team. The decision to alter the organization by adding a staff supervisor was in part made in response to the size of the new merged team.

Staff classification levels were in part linked to the level of self-management. Therefore, as the reorganization took shape, concern was expressed that some staff would be reclassified to a lower level. While no guarantees could be made, it was clear from the task analysis that current position descriptions did not clearly describe the level of skill and knowledge required of most positions. In particular, complex problem solving was now part of each position and required a higher level of knowledge than previously documented.

Lastly, staff expressed concern about the new supervisor. Their work lives would change, but would this change be for the better? The success of the reorganization depended on successfully hiring a supervisor with demonstrated managerial experience or potential to quickly grow into the new position.

IMPLEMENTATION OF ORGANIZATIONAL CHANGE

The transition to the new organizational model was relatively stress free given staff involvement throughout the planning process. All three teams now felt they were working much better together, and there was a marked improvement in the overall work climate. Newer hires in the Serials Department had also raised the department's performance level. Training had been removed from the teams, and designated trainers appointed. This included using staff from units outside the Serials Department to train staff in invoice processing.

The final transition to a supervised work unit included the following steps:

- Recruit and appoint staff supervisor.
- Merge Receiving and Ordering and Invoicing Teams into Serial Acquisitions Unit within six months after the appointment of the unit supervisor.
- Serials Cataloging Team would remain a self-directed team in the Serials Department reporting directly to the department head.
- Reassign tasks as necessary to improve processes.
- Review all job descriptions.

The new organizational model was relatively flat, with the addition of a single level of supervision for the newly formed Serials Acquisitions Unit (Figure 8.2). While a level of supervision had been added to the organization, staff expectations had not changed, and new opportunities for growth could be more easily explored.

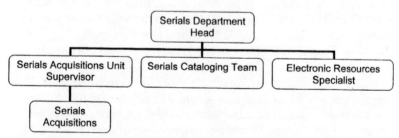

Figure 8.2.   New Organization Model, 2005

During this period, the Serials Department had become responsible for electronic resources management. The rapid growth of electronic resources during the previous five-year period has greatly impacted serials management. A new position of electronic resources specialist was created that reported directly to the department head. While this new position is responsible for many aspects of electronic resources management, the newly formed Serial Acquisitions Unit has now begun to make the transition from management of print to electronic resources.

CONCLUSION

Successful self-directed work teams cannot be created overnight. Becoming a successful self-directed work team is an evolutionary process as staff members need to be committed to taking on greater degrees of responsibility and self-management. Clearly defining and clarifying the level of self-management is crucial to success. This includes a clear definition of the role of the supervisor/manager and/or department head that is understood and accepted by all parties.

The reorganization from the traditional hierarchical organizational model to self-directed work teams reduced supervisory overhead and empowered staff to better manage their work environment and participate in the decision-making process. However, the change from the traditional model to self-directed work teams can be difficult and not easily accepted by staff accustomed to a more structured environment where individual accountability is rule based.

Any organizational assessment needs to be an ongoing process. This was the case with Penn State's Serials Department. It was important to preserve the skill sets and staff empowerment gained from the self-directed work team structure. But there was also a need to address a gap in team leadership. This was addressed by creating a new staff supervisory position with direct responsibility for management of a combined Serials Acquisitions Unit.

The transition was remarkably smooth due in large part to staff involvement and buy-in to the organizational changes. However, once the new organizational structure was announced, there were concerns regarding staff salary levels and the impact of having a new supervisor that needed to be addressed.

At this time, customer confidence in serials management, work climate, and staff skill levels have improved, allowing that there will always be room for improvement. The Serials Department is now better positioned to address new challenges, including making the successful transition from a department responsible primarily for management of print serials to a department responsible for management of print and electronic resources.

FUTURE RESEARCH

Two recommendations for future research studies are offered. The first is a longitudinal study of organizational culture in libraries before and after moving from a traditional hierarchical model to the flatter self-directed work team model. Based on the Penn State Libraries Serials Department's experience, not all individuals respond in the same manner to changes in organizational models. While extensive training was provided, skill sets and commitment to the team structure varied. Research studies that address factors such as quality of work life, leadership, and accountability before, during, and after reorganization in library technical service departments would be beneficial.

The second recommendation is a study of the role of the supervisor/manager in the team environment. The balance between the newly empowered team and the supervisor/manager, who is held accountable for the team's performance, must be clearly defined and understood. A study that involves input from team members and supervisors/managers on their perceived roles of self-management and managerial authority would be useful. In particular, it would be useful to track changes in individual beliefs on the role of the supervisor/manager before, during, and after reorganization.

NOTES

1. Monica E. Biggs, "The Exercise of Authority by Team Managers During the Implementation of Self-Directed Work Teams: A Case Study" (PhD diss., George Washington University, 1996), 2.

2. Linda I. Glassop, "The Organizational Benefits of Teams," *Human Relations* 55, no. 2 (2002): 225–249.

3. Jon R. Katzenbach and Douglas K. Smith, *The Wisdom of Teams: Creating the High-Performance Organization* (New York: HarperBusiness, 1993), 11–19.

4. Nancy M. Stanley and Lynne Branch-Brown, "Reorganizing Acquisitions at the Pennsylvania State University Libraries: From Work Units to Teams," *Library Acquisitions: Practice & Theory* 19, no. 4 (1995): 418–419.

5. Rosann Bazirjian, "After Assessment: Application of the Results of an Acquisitions Team Survey," *Library Collections, Acquisitions, and Technical Services* 25 (2001): 371–372.

6. Stanley and Branch-Brown, "Reorganizing Acquisitions," 421.

7. Susan Michie and Michael A. West, "Measuring Staff Management and Human Resource Performance in the NHS," Commission for Health Improvement, n.d., 38, www.chi.nhs.uk/eng/surveys/nss2003/Ωmichie _and_west_paper.pdf (accessed March 14, 2005).

8. Dawn L. Miller, "Managing Change: A Case Study of the Implementation of Team-Based Organizational Structures" (master's thesis, Carleton University, 1994), 15–17.

9. Stanley and Branch-Brown, "Reorganizing Acquisitions," 417–425.

10. Richard S. Wellins, William C. Byham, and Jeanne M. Wilson, *Empowered Teams: Creating Self-Directed Work Groups That Improve Quality, Productivity, and Participation* (San Francisco: Jossey-Bass, 1991), 191–222.

11. Wellins, Byham, and Wilson, *Empowered Teams*, 199–222.

12. Katzenbach and Smith, *The Wisdom of Teams*, 20–26.

13. Gretchen Spreitzer, Susan G. Cohen, and Gerald E. Ledford, "Developing Effective Self-Managing Work Teams in Service Organizations," *Group & Organization Management* 24, no. 3 (1999): 344.

14. Michie and West, "Measuring Staff Management and Human Resource Performance," 12.

15. Charles C. Manz and Henry P. Sims, "Leading Workers to Lead Themselves: The External Leadership of Self-Managing Work Teams," *Administrative Science Quarterly* 32, no. 1 (1987): 106–128.

16. Charlotte Rayner, Helge Hoel, and Cary L. Cooper, *Workplace Bullying: What We Know, Who Is to Blame, and What Can We Do?* (London: Taylor & Francis, 2002), 64.

17. Miller, "Managing Change," 13–16.

18. Miller, "Managing Change," 18–21.

19. Jenny Ellis-Newman, Haji Izan, and Peter Robinson, "Costing Support Services in Universities: An Application of Activity-Based Costing," *Journal of Institutional Research in Australasia* 5, no. 1 (1996): 75–86.

20. Klaus Ceynowa, "Activity-based Cost Management in Academic Libraries—A Project of the German Research Association," *Performance Measurement and Metrics* 1, no. 2 (2000): 99–114.

21. Katzenbach and Smith, *The Wisdom of Teams*, 45–47.

Chapter 9

Letting Go: A Reflection on Teams That Were*

John Lubans Jr.

This chapter looks back on a ten-year experiment with teams in technical services at a research university library. The author explains why and how the organization where he worked evolved from a hierarchical structure to participatory management to Total Quality Management (TQM) self-managing teams, and then reverted to the hierarchy.

Major topics include the challenges encountered along with accomplishments and failures. The author asks questions about what teams need to succeed and visits the concepts behind effective teams. He explores the technical services leader's role with an emphasis on coaching, consulting, and leading in self-managing teams.

Finally, the author relates how he would improve implementing and working with teams in technical services.

As the reader is well aware, any reflection, any memoir, is colored by what occurs *after* the event. Since giving up administrative responsibility for technical services teams, I have explored highly effective teams, like the self-managing Orpheus Chamber Orchestra, a women's basketball team, and the ramp agent teams at Southwest Airlines. Their successful teamwork influences my assessment of the technical services teams I worked with.

And as visiting professor at North Carolina Central University School of Library and Information Sciences, I explore team concepts, followership, and organizational change.

My purpose in telling this story is to demonstrate the power of administratively letting go—of creating channels for staff to seek innovative and productive ways. And to display how teams, when adequately supported and protected, with high expectations and freedom for action, generally outperform traditional structures.

WHY TEAMS?

During the late 1970s and early 1980s at the university at which I worked, the library and the technical services group began to draw unwanted attention from the university administration. To some extent it was unavoidable, due to a large payroll, some vocal dissatisfaction among students and faculty about slow turnaround times, and a large, visible backlog. And there was a perception that the library was backward, when compared to peer institutions, in automating.

Exacerbating the situation was the steady opposition by librarians to any called-for economies or simplification. That knee-jerk response pretty much kept the library under the administrative microscope. The librarians were not closed to change per se—it just had to be on their terms: more funding, more staff, and more time. The library leadership (especially the executive group of which I became a member) was seemingly unable to develop any approach other than to rationalize away criticism or to add complexity to an already overly complex process.

Prior to my appointment, the university administration had brought in time and motion consultants (with clipboards and stopwatches), to assess the efficiency of library work. The consultants' recommendations were resisted, termed *ignorant*, and otherwise ridiculed by the library staff. The reader can imagine what the T&M consultants told the university administration!

However ignorant these scientific managers might have been about the nuances of technical services (TS) work, there was no escaping library user dissatisfaction and the perception that the library was hindering the progress of a university recently deemed *hot*. Our telling the university administration that the library simply knew better was, well, self-destructive. If the library is a growing, living organism, we were closer, in administrative eyes, to the image of a growing mausoleum.

Had we responded differently, this contretemps might have been only a passing administrative pique. Instead, the library's eschewing administrative guidance aggravated an atmosphere of mutual distrust. Technical Services, the library group with the largest payroll ("a bottomless pit") and with the most problems (glacial processing times and mountainous backlogs), became an obvious reform target.

When a newly installed university president echoed the prior administration's calls for reform, the library responded as usual. The resulting standoff led to the morale busting, premature departure of the university librarian.

A new, highly recruited librarian—the provost flew to the librarian's home state to convince him to accept the job—was brought in with a specific change agenda.

After a few months on the job, the new librarian concluded that what was needed was not more, but less. Less complexity, less hierarchy, and less resistance to new ideas. His first action was to assure staff participation in decision making throughout the library, including Technical Services. All staff were permitted, indeed expected, to have an opinion and a say in decision making about streamlining and the shifting of resources. He set up monthly forums for support staff, supervisors, department heads, and frontline librarians.

The new librarian asked me to head up the TS reform effort. This was a surprise since I was the associate university librarian (AUL) for Public Services. Shortly after accepting the challenge, I realized that my lack of expertise in TS was more a plus than a minus.

Immediately after my first meeting with the TS staff, in which I told them I needed their help—I did not have the answers—the staff produced a multipage list of suggestions they had been making over several years.

This list was the first glimmer of the positive effects of uncorking years of pent-up ideas, suggestions, and improvements. Our mandated reform goals were met and exceeded, and new challenges were taken on—all in the first year. My strengths were a passionate commitment to saving the time of the user, an ability to question why we did what we did, and a strong belief that staff, given the opportunity, knew the best way to do their work.

And thanks to strong leadership covering my back, I had the opportunity to corral some of the sacred cows roaming the academic library pasture.

Following our rapid improvements through participation, we moved, naturally enough, toward a team-based structure. This was helped along by the president's encouragement of total quality management applications.

Ultimately, our success was about letting go, about turning good people loose to do the job they were fully capable of doing once free of supervisory second guessing and control.

In hindsight, we were working toward the ideals and attributes that Katzenbach and Smith identified in their research of highly effective teams. These teams demonstrate clarity about and seek positive behaviors around these elements:

Purpose/mission
Team member roles
Real work
The how
Deadlines
Support
Accountability
Interdependence

Our *actual* team work was a half-baked mix of borrowed concepts from the literature and our best thinking on what teams should be. There was no library guide to teamwork we followed. We were only vaguely aware of the Katzenbach and Smith research, so we did not instill or practice all the elements, but we did, intuitively, practice enough of them to make a difference. We made use of the pragmatic *Team Handbook* from Joiner Associates (see Scholtes, Joiner, and Streibel in the bibliography), but how many department heads read their personal copy or followed its concepts is unknown.

Indeed, our teams *were* half baked. We meant well and we achieved much, but our not fully engaging all that goes into the development of best teams did diminish effectiveness.

We had little difficulty in gathering the abundance of low-hanging fruit—those internal-to-TS processes, some redundant, that were easily merged, eliminated, or simplified. But harvesting the *high* fruit—often outside TS in walled-off orchards, surrounded by moats brimming with faculty crocodiles—would have required *all* the skills and attributes of high-achieving teams.

CHALLENGES

There is opposition to any change initiative. Jealousies and other organizational pathologies are easily aroused. They cannot be eliminated, but they can be contained. As long as there is strong leadership to protect change agents against those who wish to derail the change process, the naysayers have little influence. However, once the shield is lowered, the nitpickers, and those genetically averse to any organization other than the hierarchy—the pecking order—will have their day.

Our biggest challenges were not unique to my institution; they were inherent to the culture of research libraries. This culture was less concerned about productivity and access than it was about achieving bibliographic control. It was, and may still be, a culture where size of collection—the biggest pile of books—is the one measure of best practice.

Perhaps this focus on bibliographic control was reactive. It may have been the best we could do to cope with the bookish arms race among research libraries to add annually tons of redundant and marginal materials. I am not referring to books that might have *some* use, I am talking about the wholesale acquisition of materials that predictably would have little use—if any, ever.

Another challenge was that most of my TS peers were queasy about discussing or applying any quantitative measures to workflow. Either we did not know about the law of diminishing returns or if we did, it made no difference to how we worked. Ignoring this law, we persisted in seeking to improve on nearly error-free processing by making huge commitments of resources (time, people, and processes) in a vain attempt to achieve the last few percentage points of accuracy.

Comparable to ignoring the law of diminishing returns was our failing to appreciate complexity theory. The notion behind complexity theory is that even the smallest add-on to an existing process has implications for the total system. The tiniest twist, loop, or wrinkle adds its weight and exponentially more as its ramifications work their way through the system.

In apparent opposition to common sense, we preferred to make complex systems more complex. In reality, the less complicated the system, the less resistance in the workflow, the fewer the bottlenecks.

For me, Robert Henri, the painter, put it best: "The easiest thing is the hardest. It is harder to be simple than it is to be complex" (169).

Many of us in TS believed—perhaps still do—that simple is easy, complex is hard (and better).

I recall a regular feature at semiannual national meetings of TS directors—the tradition of having the Library of Congress's report on their achievements in cataloging.

The head of Library of Congress cataloging would recite the current year's statistics but never gave comparative figures. Had they done more or less than previous years? It did not seem to matter even though they had the world's biggest backlog.

It mattered to us a lot. Since we relied on the Library of Congress producing records, I really did want to know what their productivity was and whether they were improving on it. The faster they were at pumping out records, the faster we could catalog and get books to users.

I am not implying that research libraries are averse to statistics. Our TS had mounds of statistics—the problem was what we did with them. For the most part, we kept track of numbers to give them to outside agencies and to stick into annual reports.

We made better use of our statistics once we began to compare how we were doing year to year and, eventually, over several years. We could take genuine pride in gains achieved, and when productivity took a dive, assess how we could improve our workflow. While we rarely used TQM's advanced statistical analyses, we were not afraid to use numbers to track our progress.

One unintended consequence of a survey of workload statistics among the largest research libraries—about twenty took part—was gaining a baseline to compare ourselves to. The first survey had us at the bottom of our peer group. This was no surprise to me, but it flabbergasted those on the staff who believed our cataloging was the best. It may have been the best, but it put us at the bottom of this putative productivity index.

Several years later, at the apex of our team initiatives, we were at the top of the index.

REVISION MESS

Mess finding is that piece of problem solving where you think there is something wrong, but you are not sure what. Messes are not problems, but they generally indicate the lurking presence of a problem.

Revision qualified as a mess in my library. This business, a la Parkinson's Law, of checking someone else's work debilitated staff independence and pride in work. The revision message was clear: Staff could not be trusted. And our dedication of many hours to revision and rework took away hours and hours from getting books to the shelves.

Many staff could indeed be trusted, and revising all their work was not the answer for increased productivity. We stopped revising the work of experienced staff. New staff were trained well. Senior staff's work was revised voluntarily or revised when team leaders had reason to believe revision was needed.

LAYERS OF CONVENIENCE

As we streamlined TS, we began to peel away layers of imposed procedures. These layers of extra work, of extra steps, were added for the convenience of librarians outside TS. Often these extraordinary procedures involved double-checking, hand-copying details, and seeking and finding information so someone outside TS would feel more comfortable in making decisions. No doubt to the requestor these were insignificant demands, but when compounded, they delayed workflow.

Stopping these practices led to quicker turnaround times, but we had minimal success in getting buy-in for streamlining among people external to TS.

I recall an eye-opening meeting in which a TS support staff supervisor revealed his statistical findings about each bibliographer's workflow in book selection. His statistical charts exposed several book selectors who appeared oblivious to what happens to a system when a raft of book orders comes in on the last day of the month or during one week at the end of the year.

That meeting helped more than a few bibliographers comprehend that this practice results in an uneven distribution of work, of delayed acquisition, of backlogs—and delays in readers getting their books.

WHO'S IN CHARGE HERE?

When you move toward self-management, toward empowerment, some staff will want to know who is in charge. This was a question

we never quite resolved, and the resulting confusion around empowerment could have been lessened if we had taken the time to
talk it through. A few staff, perversely enough, thought empowerment freed them to make their own schedules, pick their own work
without talking to team leaders.

Over all, support staff gained the most from the new levels of
freedom—more elbow room. Support staff—including some that
had been sidelined for years—were instrumental in helping us
make progress, often bringing brilliant ideas and shortcuts, ideas
that revised how we did our work and gained us large savings in
resources.

A few of the former library department heads were fearless in allowing staff to think about their work and were able to adjust their
attitudes and to free up those workers, to work with them more as
colleagues and less as subordinates. While we did not solve the puz-
zle of letting go, we glimpsed enough of the positive side to believe
firmly that less control is better than too much.

The ultimate challenge was the library's being a team organization in a command and control culture, an academic bureaucracy.
People outside the library humored us in our team culture but
looked askance at the possibility of applying a similar approach in
their bailiwicks. Keeping what they had, the way they had always
had it, was their preference. We discovered, as an island of teams in
an ocean of bureaucracies, that we had to explain, repeatedly, what
we were doing and to request special exemption from hierarchical
processes, like the university's performance appraisal system. While
the parent organization persisted in hierarchical ways, we increasingly became the odd man out.

ACCOMPLISHMENTS

I've already listed the Katzenbach and Smith elements deemed essential for highly effective teams. Here is how we did on a few of the
most important elements:

In most of our TS teams *purpose/mission* was clear and understood
by each team member. For these teams, success depended on the
team's achieving the performance goals explicit in their purpose and
mission. Performance goals were measurable. They had substance
and they were achieved in a timely way. In other words, something
the team "touched" literally was changed for the better. The goal, if

clear and compelling, pulled a team forward; it drew the team toward figuring out the best way to achieve the goal. Invariably, problematic teams were weak in purpose and mission and in other of the Katzenbach and Smith variables.

While *rarely explicit* in our most successful teams, *member roles* were tacitly stated, agreed upon, and understood. However, we did not achieve enough clarity around the role of the team leader. While I compressed my role into three major functions—coaching, consulting, and leading—the roles of other team leaders were never clearly defined. Mostly, titles changed but the work relationships remained the same, so that the head of the Serials/Acquisitions Department became the leader of the Serials/Acquisitions Team.

I recall a chart from industry for self-managing work teams that showed the progression of the supervisor from the center of the team circle to the rim, and then off adrift to the side. Eventually, still afloat, the supervisor appears to be responsible—with invisible links—for *several* work teams. With the exception of my own role, most team leaders remained stuck in the center of their team, rarely becoming one of the team or moving out of that circle as a coach/consultant.

Theirs was a genuine dilemma. If not making hands-on workflow decisions or imposing an expert will on the system, what did former department heads, now team leaders, do? Understandably—given our lack of clarity and training around what team leaders were to do—most kept doing the job they had been doing, albeit less autocratically. Of course, a few believed teams were great—as long as they got to be captain!

My situation was somewhat different since I was assiduously giving away authority and responsibility, all the while coaching and consulting the former department heads. My immediate peers behaved more like the AULs of old, rather than taking on any of the roles laid out below. And there were days when even I wondered about becoming superfluous.

A less discerning and unsupportive boss might have concluded that my new job roles were not the essential drivers for what we achieved. These were my primary roles, although I retained a large amount of administrative responsibility, including monitoring the budget:

Coaching:
Helping
Challenging
Encouraging

Consulting:
Investigating new ways
Intervening
Walking about

Leading:
Eliminating barriers
Managing "hand-offs"
Recommending
Translating the vision

No question about it, TS teams could have done a better job of paying attention to the *how* of working together. These questions were rarely asked: How will we make decisions? How will we work through problems? How will we give each other feedback?

HOW MUCH RISK WILL WE TAKE?

Regrettably, our training was limited, so it never took us far enough in this essential area of team building. We focused on getting the job done and hoped for the best when it came to relationship building and effective communication, both central to building trust and confidence in performance.

Outcomes drove the team's purpose. We came to concur with Katzenbach and Smith: "Only when appropriate performance goals are set does the process of discussing the goals and the approaches to them give team members a clearer purpose and choice: they can disagree with a goal and opt out or they can become accountable" (Katzenbach and Smith, *The Discipline of Teams*, 116).

Initially, the team leaders and I set what we regarded as achievable team goals and identified who would do what and what resources it would take. The staff delivered on our expectations. Later, in keeping with our interpretation of self-managing teams, we asked team members to set their own goals. Their goals were higher each year!

Job *deadlines* were stated and respected among TS teams. Most understood that time was inelastic—gone were the days when we looked upon it as unlimited. Action, even with mistakes, was always preferred to no action with lots of analysis.

Demonstrable *support* did come from the "top"—at least during our golden years. However, we did have difficulty with the concept that the team leader was an active participant in unit teams. Some teams thought they could go off and do their own thing without discussion with a team leader or with me. While it was delusional for any team to think it had gotten a pass from being accountable to its team leader, a few did.

Some resisted the concept that teams were *accountable* to the organizational leadership. While effective teams do not set their own agenda—not even self-managing teams—some believed they could, much to my dismay. I supported maximum creative freedom for each team. They could question the basic assumptions. They could harass the sacred cows. If money was an issue, they could petition for more money and to suggest creative ways to save money. But I believe that every team needs outside guidance, needs objective feedback to keep it in sync with other teams.

Our early success was enabled by the promises made and kept by the university librarian: no layoffs, no loss of jobs, and we would get to keep any money saved through salary attrition to use for equipment and staffing in TS and in other parts of the library.

We shared our sizable gains. We followed a policy of open budgets. Salary savings were tracked monthly and a percentage assigned to TS. Team leaders reviewed monthly budget printouts and talked with me about ways to use savings. The branch libraries and public service units benefited from our streamlining with staff transfers and the purchase of equipment. We were able to implement new technological applications and address long-delayed needs—for example, retrospective conversion was funded out of salary savings and reassigned staff.

TRAINING AND DEVELOPMENT

We invested in staff training, with mixed results. Technical training for better use of the TS databases, for better use of productivity software, was generally helpful. The outcome of using university trainers for teamwork, TQM, participatory management, and organizational change was less satisfactory.

These consultants had rarely worked in teams and had only elementary ideas about TQM. External consultants were hardly better.

My suspicion was that these experts were pretty thin when it came to real experience. They talked the game but had never played it.

A scarcity of players was a problem overall—there was a lack of other team-based institutions with whom we could relate. One or two other libraries were professing team-based structures, but on closer inspection, they seemed to be working more at the emotional and attitudinal level (the how of group dynamics) than on improving the library or achieving higher productivity.

While coming up empty in much of the out-of-the-box team training, we did develop one staff development program that helped us develop camaraderie, risk taking, and creativity: adventure learning.

We offered backpacking trips, rock climbs, ropes courses, orienteering, and several "days in the woods" full of team building and problem solving. Our program was built around metaphors and designed to show new juxtapositions and possibilities. Our point was that none of us was immutably fixed in place—we were all capable of new things and new ways of working. The circle was our most obvious metaphor—it surfaced in every postadventure discussion to describe our community, how we worked together, and how we literally supported each other.

Over the course of our adventuring, about a fifth of the total library staff volunteered to take part, mostly support staff. In TS, a much larger contingent took and met the challenge. That our facilitators were two former Outward Bound instructors raised the probability of success. Their background gave them an outstanding ability to challenge us, to guide us toward teamwork, and to help us extract relevant, sometimes profound, meaning from each experience.

Our days in the woods had much to do with the success of the TS change efforts. I doubt it was coincidence that several of the people driving change in TS were active and frequent participants in outdoor learning. And, upon reflection, those days did address in candid ways the how of our working together, how we would support each other, and how we made decisions.

WHAT I WOULD DO DIFFERENTLY

Train all staff a minimum of forty hours in team concepts and practices. Make that training hands-on with opportunities to practice team leadership and team work situations. Emphasize feedback giving, question asking, and dealing with dysfunctional team leaders and members.

Experiment with different kinds of teams and with taking turns leading teams. Swap out team leaders to avoid the trap of expert control.

Cross-train team members to help other teams.

Adjust the salary infrastructure to better reflect equal levels of teamwork.

Identify the level of empowerment in teams. Make clear the roles of the team leader, the team sponsor or overseer, and other leaders.

Recognize that some staff may be averse to teams *and* be productive. Accept them as uncomfortable with the team concept but essential to getting the work out.

Jettison any system of performance appraisal—which we did. Replace it with a culture of regular and respectful feedback, well considered and timely. Annually, have a conversation with each staff member about goals and aspirations. *They* talk, you listen.

Teach critical thinking, problem recognition, and factual decision making.

Seek diplomatic solutions to conflict between TS and other teams or departments that regularly interact with TS. Build strong relationships with units outside TS. Appoint TS ambassadors to work with other units to reach mutually beneficial arrangements.

Assure fair and adequate recognition of accomplishments in TS. When gains in TS benefit other units, make sure there is recognition of the TS staff and the benefiting staff.

Confront the naysayers early on. It is a mistake to ignore negative rumors about team efforts in TS in hopes the rumormongers will go away or become reasonable as you demonstrate success. Your success is more reason for opponents to fear teams. Ignore them, and they will become more audacious.

Teach how to disagree agreeably.

CONCLUSION

In the late 1990s TS teams began to gravitate toward the traditional hierarchy. The main reason was the same as the reason we had abandoned the hierarchy a decade ago: a new university president.

The incumbent president was known for loosely holding the administrative reins, for encouraging independence and an entrepreneurial sprit. His promotion of TQM applications provided a protective shield for the library.

When he stepped down, the trustees recruited his replacement from the command and control tradition. It appeared they were seeking to dispel the "Who's in charge here?" question they might have around the prior president's style. Not long after the new president's arrival she quickly made clear her preference for the traditional model of administrative oversight—the days of proactive exploration and work innovation, at least in the library, quickly came to an end.

The incumbent librarian, hired by the previous president, realized that his preference for an innovative organization was not going to fit in in a bureaucracy. While he had been highly effective at "challenging the process and enabling others to act," these were now less important attributes. He left.

Top-down decision making and bottom-up permission seeking were once again the preferred model.

Looking back, as I write this in early 2005, during that period of four or five golden years, those "teams that were" achieved much—more than we dreamed, beyond everyone's expectations. We did *let go* and marveled at how well a TS organization of over one hundred people could climb what seemed an impossible mountain.

NOTE

*This case study looks back on a ten-year experiment with teams in technical services at Duke University.

My roles during these years were that of assistant university librarian for Public Services, then AUL for Technical Services, associate university librarian, and ultimately, deputy university librarian. In 2000, I left the university.

BIBLIOGRAPHY

Henri, Robert. *The Art Spirit: Notes, Articles, Fragments of Letters and Talks to Students, Bearing on the Concept and Technique of Picture Making and the Study of Art Generally, and on Appreciation.* New York: Harper & Row, 1984.

"'I Ain't No Cowboy; I Just Found This Hat': Confessions of an Administrator in an Organization of Self-Managing Teams," *Library Administration and Management* 10 (Winter 1996): 28–40.

Katzenbach, Jon R., and Doug K. Smith. *The Discipline of Teams: A Mindbook-Workbook for Delivering Small Group Performance.* New York: Wiley, 2001.

Kouzes, James M., and Barry Z. Posner. *The Leadership Challenge.* 3rd ed. San Francisco: Jossey-Bass, 2003.

Lubans, John. "A Reason for Rain: Hoop Lessons for Library Leaders," *Library Administration and Management* 13 (Winter 2001): 39–43.

———. "Orchestrating Success." In *People in Charge: Creating Self-Managing Workplaces,* edited by Robert Rehm, 187–197. Gloucestershire, England: Hawthorn Press, 2002.

———. "Teams in Libraries," *Library Administration and Management* 17 (Summer 2003): 144–146.

Scholtes, Peter R., Brian L. Joiner, and Barbara J. Streibel. *The Team Handbook.* 3rd ed. Madison, WI: Oriel, 2003.

Chapter 10

Implementing and Dismantling Teams in Technical Services at the University of Kentucky Libraries

Mary McLaren

The University of Kentucky Libraries adopted a self-directed management and work team structure in the mid-1990s. After operating within this model for eight years, the University Libraries are returning to the more traditional division/department model. It is anticipated that the management, leadership, and participatory skills that were developed during the team experience will carry over to the new structure as well.

Change is in the air.
What goes 'round comes 'round.
Nothing ventured, nothing gained.
If it ain't broke, don't fix it.
There are scouts, and there are settlers . . .
Let's jump on the bandwagon!

What do these maxims have in common? What are they referring to? Perhaps they are describing the various attitudes held by staff at the University of Kentucky Libraries as they proposed a change in management style in the mid-1990s.

It was during this time that the university libraries began an in-depth self-examination of their organizational model as it related to the libraries' overall mission and goals. With an eye toward improving patron services while increasing operational efficiency and effectiveness, the libraries embarked on a series of steps that ultimately led to

the adoption of a team-based management structure coupled with attendant self-directed work teams.

THE PROCESS BEGINS

The process began in the summer of 1995 when three ad hoc process
teams were created for the purpose of assessing the major processes
within the parameters of technical services, public services, and
management. Following the assessment, the process teams were
asked to submit proposals for administrative redesigns that would
improve the execution and provision of the identified processes and
services. Since this was the first exposure to formal team processes
for most of the participants, the library offered a variety of training
opportunities that addressed team building, decision making, management, quality improvement, and change. Participants learned
how to use management tools from A to P—affinity diagrams to
process flow charts, as well as others in between.[1] Participants
learned the importance of gathering and evaluating customer input.
They practiced techniques of conducting focus groups, and they designed questionnaires.

TECHNICAL SERVICES PROCESSING TEAM

The Technical Services Process Team consisted of an appointed,
trained team leader, a process consultant, a member at large, and department heads from Acquisitions, Cataloging, Collection Development, Periodicals, and Preservation. At the outset, this team adopted
a set of operational ground rules, primary among them the understanding that there would be no protection of "private turf" and all
decisions would be reached by consensus.[2]

During the course of its work, the team developed a set of goals
for the envisioned unit as well as proposed practices that would
support the accomplishment of the goals. Key themes that emerged
from the work analysis included the need to provide optimal customer service, incorporate cross-functionality into workflows,
weigh centralization/decentralization, develop and utilize staff subject expertise, and adopt the relatively new to us options of outsourcing.[3]

Per the acceptance of the Technical Services Processing Team recommendations the following year, the Technical Services Division was dissolved, and a Processing Services Team was established. It was agreed that the Technical Services reorganization would take place in phases, beginning first with the creation of a cross-functional, self-directed work team called the Monograph Processing Team.

MONOGRAPH PROCESSING TEAM

The newly created Monograph Processing Team consisted of an appointed team leader, fifteen faculty and staff, and an ad hoc facilitator who facilitated team meetings and participated in team-building workshops. The group's initial charge was to work as a team using accepted team processes and to design an organizational model for itself. Considerable amounts of time and effort were devoted to learning and applying the concepts of empowerment, participatory problem solving, and decision making by consensus. Additionally, all team members were introduced to specific management tools such as effective meeting components, data gathering techniques, and decision-making strategies.[4]

Within the designated time frame, the Monograph Processing Team developed a set of goals that supported the libraries' vision and mission statements. It designed its own organizational structure, created more efficient workflows, and assigned responsibilities to each team member. The new model incorporated more staff cross-training, more flexibility of duties, more efficient handling and processing procedures, and the utilization of some outsourced cataloging services. In accord with the team concept, the Monograph Processing Team also incorporated peer review and self-evaluation components into its annual review process.[5] Lists of the Technical Services goals and the Monograph Processing Team goals and structure criteria are included in McLaren (2001).

EVOLUTION

From 1996 through 2004, the libraries functioned under the team-based structure. Top management within the library system operated within a framework designed around seven subject-based service centers—Agriculture Information Center, Fine Arts, Law Library, Medical Center Library, Science and Engineering, Special Collections and Archives, and the William T. Young Library (Humanities, Social Sciences, and Life Sciences). As had been the case with the earlier process team participants and also with members of the Monograph Processing Team, the library sponsored a variety of team-training forums in which all library faculty and staff were encouraged to participate. The intent was to familiarize all staff at all levels with the concepts of equilateral communication and decision making, as well as team-based empowerment, change, and trust. In addition to the basic training supplied by the libraries, the Monograph Processing Team enlisted supplemental training for its members from the university's Human Resources staff who were familiar with team practice.

In 2002, while maintaining the team-based model, a smaller scale administrative reorganization that affected various Processing Services work teams took place within the William T. Young Library. As a result of this reorganization, Collection Development merged with Monograph Processing to form a new unit called the Collection Services Team. Serials joined the Information Services Team, Preservation and Special Projects reported directly to the Young Library director, and three staff members were transferred from Monograph Processing to the Electronic Resources Team to catalog and perform database maintenance for the ever-increasing quantity of electronic resources.

A NEW ADMINISTRATOR

Following the retirement of the director of libraries in 2002 and a one-year interim period under the leadership of an appointed acting director, July 2003 brought a new leader to the top post, which had been renamed dean of libraries. The dean of libraries arrived on the scene eager to understand everything about the university libraries—their vision, mission, goals and plans, their policies, procedures, and processes. She set out to learn all this, as well as the goals and aspirations of the individuals who made up the library community. She met individually with all library faculty and staff members, asking them to explain their areas of responsibility and soliciting their ideas for improvement. She visited every work area to learn about and see firsthand the processes and workflows in place. She met with each library committee to learn about the work it was charged to do. She met weekly with the service center team leaders regarding administrative matters, as had been past custom.

In January 2004, the dean held a Reorganization Retreat in which 35 library faculty and staff participated. The dean shared her impressions of the current state of the organization followed by a broad outline of what she foresaw in a future organization.

During the remainder of the day, participants identified attributes that they desired in an organization as well as key work processes. These processes focused on work that directly serves patrons, adds value and makes a difference for students and faculty, and is critical to the mission of the library and the university.

Following the retreat, the dean established the Reorganization Working Group (RWG), which consisted of five faculty and two staff members. The group was charged with developing one or two user-centered organizational macromodels. Assisted by the library's consultant, the RWG worked for several months on the development of its model. Adopting a user perspective, group members read background materials, examined models used by benchmark libraries, conducted focus groups with university library faculty and staff, and solicited input from all employees via the RWG website. Members examined workflows related to what users want and deconstructed them to the level of the tasks involved. These tasks were later regrouped into broader groups called clusters, and the clusters were then grouped into macrolevel groups called collaboratives. The RWG followed a route of activities described by Brown University Libraries as *process mapping* as its starting point with the work processes. Process mapping starts with the user, focuses on outcomes, and describes "what the work is that benefits the users, not *how* the work gets done or *who* does it."[6]

In May 2004, the Reorganization Working Group presented its proposed macromodel, approved by the dean, to the library at large. Presented in the form of a Venn diagram, the model consisted of six process-based collaboratives, each depicted with its designated outcomes, the collaboratives intersecting one another to show the interdependence and interoperability of each with the whole. The model of the Collections and Technical Services collaborative presented at this time depicted the following outcomes: Acquisitions, Cataloging and Metadata, Collection Development Administration, Database Integrity, Electronic Resource Coordination, Federal Documents, Serials, and Special Projects. The completed model shows Research and Development at the central core of the design to indicate that this concept should be embraced by all employees in all collaboratives.[7] An accompanying narrative document describes the mission and the outcomes expected from each collaborative.[8]

LEADER SELECTION

Once the collaboratives and their attendant work outcomes had been formulated and approved, it was time to assign a leader to each of the collaboratives. The dean of libraries distributed a list of critical skills and competencies that a collaborative leader should possess. She cited the Association of Southeastern Research Libraries' document, "Shaping the Future: ASERL's Competencies for Research Librarians,"[9] as a starting point for the selection of the leaders. Each library faculty and staff member was invited to submit nominations for the collaborative leaders. Self-nominations were also accepted. A Leader Screening Committee was appointed to facilitate the selection process.

Each nominee who wished to be considered as a candidate for a leader position was required to submit a two-page vita and written responses to a series of questions. The submitted documents were posted on the library's website for review by the entire staff. Nominees were interviewed by the Leader Screening Committee and by the dean of libraries. Each candidate presided over a question-and-answer session open to the full library faculty and staff. Staff were encouraged to submit evaluative comments about each candidate to the Screening Committee and the dean. Upon consideration of the candidate's performance in each activity and review of the peer comments, the Screening Committee submitted a written evaluation and recommendation to the dean for each candidate. The final step in this process was the dean's appointment of a leader for each collaborative.

FINAL STEPS

Employee Assignment

Now that the two-tier model was presented, an employee assignment process was announced. Every library employee below the rank of associate dean was required to complete and submit a pair of employment preference forms. One form was a chart format on which the employee was to check his or her first, second, and third (optional) preference of collaborative/cluster in which to work. The other form was a narrative that posed questions for each of the preferred choices asking what aspects of the collaborative/cluster were of interest, what the employee considered to be the employee's ideal job, and how the employee's knowledge, skills, and interests would contribute to the work and outcomes of the collaborative.

A Further Refinement

Upon presenting this organization model to the libraries, the dean announced that the libraries' organization would be based on divisions and departments instead of collaboratives or teams. The first tier of the model, represented as collaboratives in the RWG model, were to become divisions; the second tier of clusters, or work outcomes, would become departments; and the collaborative leaders would be assigned the title of associate dean.

Work Redesign Teams

As the libraries neared the end of the planning period, one additional process remained to be done before the final model would be put into place. The dean created small groups called Work Redesign Teams to work on the second tiers (department level) of the model. Each team was instructed to determine and map the essential work processes that needed to occur within the collaborative (division) that they were reviewing for the collaborative's various kinds of input to result in the desired kinds of output. The Collections and Technical Services (CTS) Work Redesign Team worked within the parameters of centralizing functions wherever possible and utilized a triage approach that called for starting work at the lowest appropriate level and shifting to a problem-solving level when necessary. Areas of overlap with other collaboratives were recognized, such as coordinating CTS linkserver activities with Information Technology and transferring budget information from the Office of the Dean to CTS. Transition issues that needed to be considered were duly noted, as well as additional resources that would be required. The CTS Work Design Group's recommendation resulted in a reduction in the number of second-tier levels from eight, as proposed in the previous model, to three, these three being Access Record Management, Acquisitions, and Collection Development. The second column in Table 10.1 reflects the

Table 10.1. Organization Model

Service Center Teams (Libraries) [1996–2004]	Divisions (Departments) [2005–present]
• Agriculture Information Center	• Access and Delivery (Circulation, Interlibrary Loan, Storage)
• Fine Arts Libraries (Architecture, Art, Music)	• Collections and Technical Services (Access Record Management, Acquisitions, Collection Development)
• Law Library	• Information Technology (Desktop Support, Integrated Library System, Network, Server, and Web Administration)
• Medical Center Library	• Law Library (decentralized)
• Physical Science and Engineering Libraries (Chemistry, Engineering, Geology, Maps, Mathematics, Physics, Transportation)	• Medical Center Library (decentralized)
• Special Collections and Archives	• Office of the Dean (Administrative Services, Assessment, Business Services, Development, Human Resources, Marketing)
• William T. Young Library (Humanities, Life Sciences and Social Sciences Collections)	• Research and Education (Academic Liaisons, Interdisciplinary Information Literacy, Reference Commons)
	• Special Collections and Digital Programs (Archives, Digital Programs, Oral History Program, Preservation, Special Collections Library)

organization model that was implemented by the University of Kentucky Libraries in January 2005.

HOW IS THE NEW MODEL DIFFERENT?

How is the new division/department hierarchical model that was implemented in 2005 different from the service center team model that had served as the libraries' umbrella since 1996? The first major difference is the focal point around which the divisions are defined.

The service center teams were formed around the concept of physical libraries—the subject matter of their collections, the subject expertise of their librarians and staff, and the clientele they served. The divisions, on the other hand, are designed according to the type of work performed within the unit and the resultant "outcomes" that are produced for the benefit of the users. The service center model featured the decentralization of most work processes, whereas the division model generally calls for centralization, with exceptions being made for the Law and Medical Center libraries.

Relating specifically to technical services functions, the former service centers were expected to develop technical service expertise among their own staff, assuming responsibility for managing their budgets as well as ordering, receiving, and cataloging their own materials. In reality, some of the staff did not receive adequate technical services training under the supervision of experienced personnel, but were, however, still assigned technical services responsibilities in addition to their public services tasks. Under the division model, technical services functions will be administered centrally within the Collections and Technical Services Division, with some staff performing these functions in separate library locations.

Another primary difference between the two models is the application of cross-training and flexibility. The team model strongly supports the concept of staff cross-training, thereby increasing the breadth of knowledge among team members and promoting flexibility. Staff in the smaller libraries might be trained in both technical and public services, thereby enabling them to perform a spectrum of duties as needed within their service center. The service center team concept, which formed a supportive bond between multiple libraries, lent itself well to staff temporarily assisting other libraries within their team in times of need. Temporary staff shortages and special project needs were often accommodated by volunteers within a supporting administrative team.

The division model, on the other hand, promotes the development of deeper levels of knowledge and expertise among a more consolidated group of individuals. With improved communication, a more consistent understanding and application of system-wide procedures and standards is expected to result.

The decision-making process reflects another major difference between the two systems. Team management is characterized by a participatory, consensus-based decision-making process. All team members are involved in defining, discussing, analyzing, proposing solutions, and making decisions, with each member's contribution carrying the same weight as every other member's. Ideally, final decisions are reached by consensus. Hierarchical management decision making may be as inclusive or exclusive as the unit head desires. Group participation may be encouraged, but the final decision rests with the unit head.

Accountability is yet another variable that differs between the two plans. Accountability within teams rests with the team members. Accountability within a hierarchical structure rests with the person in charge of the task.

Because of the group dynamics inherent in strong teams, the allegiance of team members to their team can prove to be very strong. This can, in some instances, prevent team members from seeing the "big picture," resulting in their being responsive to only the needs of their own team. Members of hierarchical units, on the other hand, might not be as susceptible to this type of "tunnel vision" because they work more independently, the work they produce is distributed to a user base beyond their immediate sphere, and their responsibility is system-wide.

Positive feelings of ownership and "buy-in" toward team-generated and team-accepted goals and projects are experienced by team members who have been actively involved in the project—from design, through implementation, to completion. Members of a more autonomous unit might not experience the same degree of ownership if their personal involvement is of a lesser degree.

Personal motivation of team members may prove to be either strong or weak. They may contribute as highly as possible because they want a team project to succeed or because of their own self-motivation. Then again, team members who lack both self-motivation and team dedication may opt for minimal productivity because they believe that others on the team will take up their slack. Conversely, members of a hierarchical unit are independently responsible for their own output, which must result from their individual motivation.

WHAT WORKED, WHAT DID NOT WORK, AND WHAT SHOULD HAVE BEEN DONE DIFFERENTLY

Self-directed management and work teams have proven to be successful in a variety of settings. At the University of Kentucky Libraries, the results of the team experience are mixed. Some aspects of the team experience have proven to be positive and others less than satisfactory. The following list reflects some opinions voiced by Technical Services personnel regarding the positive and negative aspects of their team experiences at the university libraries.

What Worked Well

- High degree of cooperation among work teams within an administrative unit
- Opportunities to participate and contribute
- Diverse expertise brought to problem-solving activities
- Diversity of views during brainstorming sessions
- Cross-training
- Flexibility
- Empowerment
- Working as a group on projects
- Team members taking ownership and buy-in to solutions
- More effective meetings
- Members being valued because of their contributions, not their rank
- Designing complex processes
- Gratifying to work on successful projects
- Problem-solving and project-oriented activities worked the best
- Working for a cohesive whole
- Processes were not fragmented by individuals doing just "their" job
- Excellent communication between units within the team
- Units worked cooperatively to develop workflows and procedures
- Autonomy allowed things to get done at lower levels
- Faster turnaround times with fewer hand-offs
- New perspective to the library system

What Did Not Work Well

- Distributed service centers
- Uneven and incomplete implementation of teams across the library system
- Unequal and incomplete training (for different teams, for members within the same team, and for newly hired staff)

- Long-term interest and support of teams from top administration waned
- Lack of checks and balances regarding team operations
- Confusion about who could make decisions
- Unclear parameters relating to personnel issues
- Some teams became territorial and did only what was good for their own team
- Competition, instead of partnerships, developed between some teams
- Reaching consensus is time consuming
- Some teams "did their own thing," ignoring standards
- Lack of willingness by some to participate in team functions that provided feedback to higher-level teams
- Daily workflow and routine tasks did not lend themselves well to the multifunctional team structure
- Small decisions involved too many people and became tedious
- Some departments changed their name to "team," but nothing else changed
- Some team leaders did not follow established team process

What Should Have Been Done Differently?

Responding to a recent survey (see the appendix), Technical Services staff voiced their opinions about a number of scenarios that, had they been present or applied somewhat differently, might have produced more positive results. These include

- Complete implementation of the team structure from top to bottom and across the board
- Commitment from top administration to support team structure for the long run
- Equal training in team process for all teams and all team members, including new hires
- Systematic review of team operation with a mechanism in place for making adjustments as needed
- Methodologies suited to non-problem-solving situations, such as daily operations
- University Human Resources policy that adequately rewarded successful team players through the annual performance evaluation process

- Clearly delineated lines of communication and authority
- A strategy in place for team leader turnover
- Some common goals for all teams to work toward together
- Clear and open communication explaining the rationale behind directives

CONCLUSION

The University of Kentucky Libraries moved from a hierarchical division/department management structure to an equilateral team structure in 1996. In 2005, the libraries were transitioning back to the former model. Each management style has its own particular strengths and weaknesses; each may be suitable for particular environments yet unsuitable for others.

The team experience at the University of Kentucky Libraries proved to be unequal in its application and unequal in its success. Teams in which all members received adequate training in team processes and task processes were more successful than teams that provided inadequate training to their members. The library did not provide for a system-wide review of team operations, and this resulted in variant interpretations of the team process within the system.

A major impediment to the successful implementation of the team structure within the University of Kentucky Libraries is the university's administrative structure as a whole. Being a non-team-based institution, the university's performance review and reward system does not accommodate the concept of team performance. In effect, its current system, which results in individuals competing for salary raises, is counterproductive to the concept of team reward.

Equally important, however, may be the fact that the University Libraries did not consistently demonstrate an unwavering and long-term commitment that is necessary to support the development, operation, and improvement of their teams. For teams to succeed, they must be provided continuous support in the forms of a suitable governance structure, customized policies, and adequate resources. For teams to succeed, the library must develop and revise procedures, as needed, to meet the needs of team operation. Moreover, the library must provide for the development and performance of its entire staff within the team construct.

In conclusion, the team structure can be effectively implemented within library and technical services settings. Its subsequent successful subsistence, however, requires thorough, consistent, and continuous attention, support, and review.

APPENDIX: SURVEY QUESTIONS

TEAM STRUCTURE IN TECHNICAL / PROCESSING / COLLECTION SERVICES

I. UK LIBRARIES

1. What do / did you like about working within the team structure of the UK Libraries, and why?

_____

_____

_____

_____

_____

2. What do / did you not like about working within the team structure of the UK Libraries, and why?

_____

_____

_____

_____

_____

II. TECHNICAL / PROCESSING / COLLECTION SERVICES

1. What aspects of technical / processing / collection services work do / did work well within the team structure, and why?

_____

_____

_____

_____

2. What aspects of technical / processing / collection services do / did not work well within the team structure, and why?

_____

_____

III. UNIT WORK

1. What aspects of your unit's operation do / did work well within the team structure, and why?

---

2. What aspects of your unit's operation do / did not work well within the team structure, and why?

IV. WHAT MIGHT HAVE WORKED BETTER?

---

1. What changes in the UK Libraries team structure, had they been implemented, might have resulted in improved work processes, and why?

---

2. What changes in the UK Libraries team structure, had they been implemented, might have resulted in an improved workplace, and why?

V. OTHER THOUGHTS OR COMMENTS?

_____

_____

_____

_____

_____

Your name: _____

Type of work performed (Indicate all that apply):
Acquisitions—monos or serials; Binding; Cataloging—monos or serials; Collection development; Database management; Digitization;
Electronic resources licensing; Labeling; Preservation; Receiving—
monos or serials; Reformatting; Other _____

Approximate length (in years) of team work experience: _____

Please return completed form to Mary McLaren, Administrative Services, 1-85 W T Young Library, -0456 before October 15. (e-mail:
mclaren@email.ukty.edu, FAX: 257-8379). Phone: 257-0500, x2086

THANKS SO MUCH FOR SHARING YOUR VIEWS!!!

NOTES

1. McLaren, "Team Structure," 358–359.
2. McLaren, "Team Structure," 359.
3. McLaren, "Team Structure," 361.
4. McLaren, "Team Structure," 363.
5. McLaren, "Team Structure," 364.
6. Brown University Libraries, "Process Mapping," 2001.
7. University of Kentucky Libraries, "UK Library Organization Model,"
2004.
8. University of Kentucky Libraries, "Reorganization Working Group,"
2004.
9. Association of Southeastern Research Libraries, "Shaping the Future:
ASERL's Competencies for Research Librarians," 2000.

BIBLIOGRAPHY

Association of Southeastern Research Libraries. "Shaping the Future:
ASERL's Competencies for Research Librarians." 2000. www.aserl.org/

statements/competencies/competencies.htm (accessed February 27, 2005).

Brown University Libraries. "Process Mapping." 2001. www.brown.edu/ Facilities/University_Library/MODEL/LTMG/maps/intro.html (accessed February 27, 2005).

Brown University Libraries. "Process Maps Revised, October 2001." 2001. www.brown.edu/Facilities/University_Library/MODEL/LTMG/maps2/ index.htm (accessed February 27, 2005).

McLaren, Mary. "Team Structure: Establishment and Evolution within Technical Services at the University of Kentucky Libraries," *Library Collections, Acquisitions, and Technical Services* 25 (2001): 357–369.

University of Kentucky Libraries. "Reorganization Working Group." 2004. www.uky.edu/Libraries/reorgmh.doc (accessed February 27, 2005).

———. "Reorganization Working Group Report to the Dean of Libraries; Phase I: Macro-Model Development, Feb 11–June 7, 2004" (unpublished report). 2004.

———. "UK Library Organization Model." 2004. www.uky.edu/Libraries/ orgmodel.doc (access February 27, 2005).

Part 4

SPECIAL-PURPOSE TEAMS

Chapter 11

And They Lived Happily Ever After: Findings from the Penn State University Libraries' AV Workflow Process Improvement Team

Robert B. Freeborn and Ann H. Dodd

In 2003 the Pennsylvania State University Libraries established a process improvement team to review the entire workflow for processing MediaTech materials. The team benchmarked with other institutions, documented the current workflow, examined possible changes, and then made recommendations. When the team started its work in December 2003, three different parts of the organization used two catalogs and two technical systems to serve Music/AV patrons with a process that averaged fifty-five workdays from order placement to completion of cataloging for user access. Through implementation of the team's recommendations the cycle time for the process has been reduced by one-third and as of late 2004–early 2005 averages just seventeen workdays.

This cycle time reduction was accomplished without changes in personnel, technical systems, or hardware. The process of serving Music/AV patrons still requires the use of two technical systems by three different parts of the organization, but the three parts of the organization now see themselves as part of one unified process. Group cohesion and group performance have both been enhanced. Team members now have a greater awareness of user issues. Interestingly, it appears that the group's use of a structured communication process proved to be just as important as the final results.

In December 2003, a process improvement team was cosponsored by the director of the Media and Technology Support Services (Media-Tech) and the head of Cataloging Services at the Pennsylvania State

University Libraries. They were asked to review the entire acquisitions and cataloging process for MediaTech materials and decide where improvements could be made. The team's makeup included those Acquisitions, Cataloging, and MediaTech staff members directly involved in the MediaTech workflow. It was important to include staff in the decision-making process so that their voice could be reflected in the final recommendations. To this group were added the Music/AV cataloging librarian as chair, and a facilitator from Penn State's Office of Planning and Institutional Assessment. The facilitator kept the team focused on the tasks at hand, as well as serving as a go-between with the cosponsors in case questions arose.

The team's charge was to

1. Review and document the current ordering, receiving, cataloging, and processing; workflow(s) for video, film, and DVD (or media) materials that the libraries acquire;
2. Evaluate the effectiveness of the current workflow;
3. Review a series of issues supplied by the cosponsors (these issues will be addressed in "Outcomes and Recommendations");
4. Benchmark with other academic institutions that use both online catalogs and the Medianet database software to manage media;
5. Make recommendations for changes to the current workflow in order to
   a. Streamline the processes and maximize their effectiveness;
   b. Avoid duplication of effort;
   c. Maximize the timeliness of processing the materials.

There were also three constraints put on the team's process and recommendations:

1. The solution cannot include or require financial expenditures or additional staff.
2. The solution cannot compromise Cataloging Services' cataloging standards. Cataloging Services adheres to national standards through the use of the Anglo-American Cataloguing Rules (AACR), Library of Congress Rule Interpretations (LCRI), Library of Congress Subject Headings (LCSH), and the Machine-Readable Cataloging (MARC) data-tagging format. MediaTech, however, utilizes local cataloging rules and subject thesauri.

3. The solution cannot require software purchases to replace Medianet. MediaTech asserts that Medianet contains an excellent media-booking module, superior to that of Penn State's current online catalog (Sirsi Unicorn), and they don't want to lose it.

In addition, the cosponsors included three measures of success for the project:

1. A streamlined process with fewer steps and/or handoffs.
2. The ability for Cataloging Services to provide full original cataloging when required.
3. A solution that provides for backup staffing for all involved.

The team met for four half days at a neutral location on Penn State's University Park campus to work things out. They then presented their recommendations to their cosponsors, and, upon approval, implemented a six-month trial period. The remainder of this chapter examines the methodology used by the team, the findings they achieved, the recommendations based on those findings, and the outcomes of their implementation.

BACKGROUND

In 1993, the Pennsylvania State University Libraries acquired MediaTech (formerly Audiovisual Services) from the university's Office of Continuing and Distance Education. First created in the 1940s, this department maintains both a film/video collection and a media equipment support service. The collection of 16 mm films, videos, and DVDs is housed in a building separate from that of the library and is cataloged using the Medianet software package. Materials ordered for MediaTech were received by the libraries' Acquisitions Services department, and then sent directly to their final location. The staff at MediaTech would then view the item and catalog it according to their requirements, including a lengthy summary note that is usually included on catalog records. Finally, an electronic surrogate would be sent to the library's Cataloging Services department so that the Music/AV Cataloging Team could add the item to the online catalog.

This situation had caused many problems for our users. The first related to availability. Often the item would appear available according to the MediaTech records, while the online catalog would still show it as "In Process." It depended on how long it took for the surrogate to be created, sent, and then processed. The second problem concerned accessibility. A comparison of bibliographic records in Medianet and the online catalog for the same DVD reflects the numerous ways that the databases differ in providing access (appendix A). One very important difference concerns the subject thesaurus. Medianet records utilize a homegrown list of keywords, while online catalog records use Library of Congress subject headings. Finally, there was the question of local policy. Because physical items were never sent to Cataloging for processing, the Music/AV Cataloging Team was unable to perform original cataloging on those materials for which there wasn't any copy in the national utilities. This left the catalog scattered with numerous minimal-level records that have caused much consternation and subsequent cleanup.

These problems resulted in complaints from Public Services personnel and patrons, and subsequently the formation of the AV Workflow Process Improvement Team.

BENCHMARKING AND LITERATURE SURVEY

A search of the professional literature on the topic, coupled with queries to selected media electronic lists, proved to be of rather limited assistance. While there are well-written articles on quality in cataloging in general[1] and video cataloging practices in particular,[2] none seemed to really address this particular situation. Recent works on the reorganization of Penn State University Libraries' Cataloging Services department helped to provide background on its current environment,[3, 4] but there is nothing similar that addresses the history and evolution of the MediaTech department, or similar organizations at other institutions.

A question to the Media-L (Media-L@listserv.binghamton.edu) and VideoLib (VideoLib@library.berkeley.edu) electronic lists asking if libraries that maintained media databases in both Medianet and another database/online catalog attempted to duplicate the holdings of one within the other met with limited response. Those who replied stated that their institutions or agencies had merged all their media holdings into just one database, either in Medianet or their online catalog.

PROCESS PHASE AND METHODS

Penn State has considerable experience with process improvement and has sponsored a formal continuous quality improvement initiative since the early 1990s through the Office of Planning and Institutional Assessment reporting to the provost. This office in 1999 introduced a structured group process improvement model they call the Fast Track Improvement Model.[5] Fast Track is adapted from the Fast Cycle Change model[6] that has been used to achieve dramatic cycle time reduction for processes ranging from clinical drug trials to article writing to hiring.

Before starting the use of the fast track model, many of Penn State's improvement teams met for one to two hours a week over a period of several months to complete the design phase of their work. The longer duration of the project sometimes meant that the team's momentum was interrupted due to changes in personnel, policies, funding, technology, and so on. The fast track model differs from the traditional team approach in two ways. First, the actual time spent in team meetings is compressed from several months' duration to less than one month. Second, from the start there is a greater emphasis on ensuring successful implementation. Figure 11.1 illustrates the fast track improvement model.

The initiation phase of the fast track model takes place prior to actual team meetings. The AV workflow team was started during fall 2003 through the efforts of the associate dean of the libraries after stakeholder concerns with the process were brought to her attention. She worked with three other individuals (the team facilitator and two team sponsors) to select the focus for the project, create a project plan, and identify a working group. In keeping with the fast track model's emphasis on implementation, measures of success were identified, and the phases of the process were identified. A team was selected with individuals representing each phase of the process since these were the people who would most likely be responsible for implementation.

The design phase of the project (steps 2 and 3 of Figure 11.1) took place during a concentrated period of four half days spread over a period of two weeks in early December 2003. The facilitator guided the team through the steps required to improve the process, starting with the use of a flowchart to confirm the current process. Creation of a flowchart often helps groups to better understand each other's work,[7]

Fast Track Improvement Model

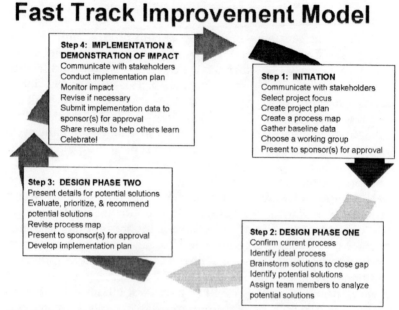

Step 4: IMPLEMENTATION & DEMONSTRATION OF IMPACT
Communicate with stakeholders
Conduct implementation plan
Monitor impact
Revise if necessary
Submit implementation data to sponsor(s) for approval
Share results to help others learn
Celebrate!

Step 1: INITIATION
Communicate with stakeholders
Select project focus
Create project plan
Create a process map
Gather baseline data
Choose a working group
Present to sponsor(s) for approval

Step 3: DESIGN PHASE TWO
Present details for potential solutions
Evaluate, prioritize, & recommend potential solutions
Revise process map
Present to sponsor(s) for approval
Develop implementation plan

Step 2: DESIGN PHASE ONE
Confirm current process
Identify ideal process
Brainstorm solutions to close gap
Identify potential solutions
Assign team members to analyze potential solutions

Figure 11.1.   Fast Track Improvement Model

and this was no exception. Interestingly, when the team initiated the design phase of the project, the MediaTech workflow was considered by team members to be three separate processes conducted by Acquisitions, MediaTech, and Cataloging. Three separate flowcharts were created that illustrated the parts of the process conducted by each of the three offices, and separate timelines for each part of the process were identified. This illustrated the need to help all members of the team broaden their understanding of the interdependencies. After creating a separate map of the three parts of the process, the team discussed opportunities for improvement that would align the current process with the ideal situation. Forty-four items of information were needed by at least one of the three areas as they conducted their part of the process. Of these, 71 percent were needed by more than one area. This helped the team to identify common ground. Two of the three areas needed sixteen of the forty-four items (36 percent), and all three areas needed another sixteen of the items. Appendix B includes a full listing of information requirements.

After the team identified common ground through the discussion of information requirements, the current process time was identified within each of the three areas. The team then studied the flowcharts to identify opportunities to reduce bottlenecks, rework, and wait time. The need for each step in the process was discussed, and potential solutions were identified. Between meetings team members researched the details of each of the potential solutions and then presented these to team members for evaluation and prioritization. It was determined that a change in the sequence of activities would be the most fruitful way to reduce the cycle time.

OUTCOMES AND RECOMMENDATIONS

Six Recommended Changes

The team identified six major changes to meet their charge. These included the following:

1. MediaTech materials will be routed first to the Music/AV Cataloging Team for processing.
2. The materials will then be shipped directly to MediaTech staff via special containers.
3. MediaTech staff will update the catalog record with local information and a summary note (520 field).
4. The Medianet database will be made more visible on the libraries' web pages.
5. MediaTech will provide public access to their local subject thesaurus via their website.
6. To ensure appropriate MediaTech backup staffing, retention of open staff positions is recommended.

Recommendations were presented to sponsors, and five of six were approved. Backup staffing for MediaTech was achieved through cross-training rather than retention of open staff positions.

Response to Stakeholder Questions

The team also presented to sponsors a response to questions that had been received from stakeholders, as follows:

1. How can the workflow be modified so that the Music/AV Cataloging Team can do full original cataloging when needed? All

materials will now go directly from Acquisitions to the Music/AV Cataloging Team.

2. How do the two groups handle different/alternative titles? This issue is system dependent. MediaTech will list title variations in Medianet annotation.

3. How can we streamline the workflow? Steps have been re-ordered to increase efficiency. See appendix C.

4. How do we handle multiple formats and multiple copies of items? This issue is driven both by system requirements and nationally accepted cataloging standards. This issue will be handled through increased/improved communication and training.

5. Is the process as timely as it can be? After review of the current process, the team felt this area could be improved upon and has made recommendations as referenced in appendix C.

6. Can we eliminate any duplication of effort, for example, searching for catalog copy? Yes. See appendix C for proposed procedural changes.

7. How can we achieve full cataloging in the CAT as soon as possible? See appendix C for proposed procedural changes.

8. Do both MediaTech and Cataloging have staffing backups so that the absence of someone doesn't restrict processing? MediaTech will need to explore retention of open positions and/or current staffing assignments to fulfill the charge. Cataloging is sufficiently staffed to ensure backup.

9. What do our users need in terms of a summary note (520 in the online catalog record), and who should write the summary note? MediaTech and the Music AV Cataloging Team will work collaboratively to create summary notes that meet both national standards and client needs.

10. How are subject headings assigned, and should there be any coordination between Medianet and Sirsi? This is system driven. Subject headings in the online catalog are based on Library of Congress subject headings. Medianet subject headings are based on a locally established thesaurus. MediaTech will publish this thesaurus via the web and will entertain requests to expand or modify this thesaurus.

11. What should we do about media materials housed at Media-Tech that are not in the online catalog? This will need to be a retrospective conversion catalog project with priority and

staffing to be negotiated with the Music/AV Cataloging Team and MediaTech.

12. What is the best way of informing Cataloging when an item has been withdrawn? Electronic notification will be sent to the Music/AV Cataloging Team at the time a title is withdrawn.

13. Are we appropriately documenting the existence (or lack of) public performance rights in Medianet and the online catalog? No. This will be addressed by training MediaTech staff to input appropriate restriction(s) on MediaTech Collection items in the online catalog. Non-MediaTech Collection items will need to be addressed by the Music/AV Cataloging Team in the future.

14. Why do the university libraries and MediaTech differ in their physical processing of videos? This issue is driven by client, system, and location and cannot be addressed by the team at this time.

IMPLEMENTATION

Reduced Cycle Time

The redesigned process has exceeded expectations for improvement. One of the team's measures of success was to achieve a streamlined process with fewer steps and handoffs. Figure 11.2 illustrates the cycle time reduction that has been achieved to date. During 2003, before the team started its work, patron concerns were not being addressed, and the workflow took an average of 141 days. Awareness

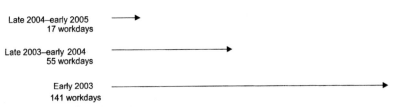

Total Elapsed Time from Placement of Order to Completion of Cataloging for User Access

Late 2004–early 2005
17 workdays

Late 2003–early 2004
55 workdays

Early 2003
141 workdays

Figure 11.2. Cycle Time Reduction

of user concerns built during 2003 and this attention may have contributed to the one-third cycle time reduction during 2003. In late 2003–early 2004 (immediately following the team's design phase but before recommendations were implemented) the workflow was an average of 55 workdays. A year later, in early 2005, the overall cycle time for the process has been reduced by almost one-third again, and it now takes an average of 17 workdays from the time an order is placed until the item is cataloged and ready for user access.

Enhanced Collaboration

At the start of the project, two catalogs and two technical systems were in use by three different parts of the organization. These areas had different standards and different clientele. When the team started the design phase in December 2003, there was no cohesion within the group, hence the separation and mapping of each of the three parts of the overall process.

The use of the fast track process helped ensure that the team was formed in a manner consistent with best practices. Two downfalls of teamwork are unclear goals and unclear roles.[8] Within the Music/AV workflow team the goals were clearly delineated, as were the roles of the sponsors, leaders, facilitator, and team members. The team used well-defined decision procedures and identified their solutions based on data. Research has shown that the use of a structured communication process enhances group performance.[9, 10, 11] At the first session in December 2003 the team identified several communication ground rules that were reinforced by the facilitator throughout the design phase of the process. Ground rules included the following:

- Maintain confidentiality
- Focus on the charge
- Respect each other's opinions
- Document the decisions
- Honesty
- Get some verbal input from everyone regarding a discussion or decision
- Don't take things personally/don't be offended when judgment is questioned

- Be sure everyone agrees with the "take-aways" from meetings (agrees with decisions)
- Positive attitude
- Be prepared and on time
- Don't assume that what "has been" needs to remain the same
- Active listening and communication

During 2004 as the team implemented the new process, it became clear that group cohesion and performance had been enhanced. When the team met in early 2005 to discuss implementation results, members referred to one process rather than three, stating, "It really wasn't working." Members stated that they had greater awareness of user issues and declared that mapping the process was critical. As one person said, "Once we saw all the steps it was pretty easy to re-order them."

CONCLUSION

The work of the AV Workflow Process Improvement Team has proven many important points from the continuous quality improvement (CQI) standpoint. The first is that the benefits of performing such an exercise far outweigh the cost in employee time. The second is that computer programming or new hardware and software aren't always the solution to processing problems. Finally, it can help employees from different work cultures to pull together on a common problem and reach a united solution.

APPENDIX A: SAMPLE MEDIANET
AND OPAC CATALOG RECORDS

Medianet Record

Title	2001, a Space Odyssey (92306)
Physical	Color; Captioned; 148 minutes
Copyrighted	1968
Distributor	Amazon.com (*AMAZON)
Audience	High School, College, Adult (SCA)
Collection	AVS

Synopsis	Digitally restored and remastered 2001 edition of the science fiction classic which moves from the pre-historic birth of intelligence toward the emergence of man as pure thought somewhere in the future. DVD features English and French language soundtracks and English, French, Spanish, and Portuguese subtitles. Written by Stanley Kubrick and Arthur C. Clarke. Produced and directed by Stanley Kubrick. No public performance rights. Classroom instruction and home use permitted. Closed captioned.
Subjects	Feature films, Science-fiction; Films, Historic / History of; French-language films; Arts and Communications (CART); Foreign-Language Media (CFOR)
Note	NO PUBLIC PERFORMANCE RIGHTS

OPAC Record (as it appears in OCLC)

Type: g ELvl: ISrce: d   Audn: Ctrl: Lang: eng
BLvl: m Form: GPub:Time: 148   MRec: Ctry: cau
Desc: a TMat: v   Tech: l   DtSt: p   Dates: 2001, 1968

040	OQX $c OQX $d MNM $d EMU $d ONU $d OCL $d JED
007	v $b d $d c $e v $f a $g i $h z
020	0790760118
024 10	012569553927
028 42	65539 $b Warner Home Video
041 1	eng $a fre $h eng $b spa $b por $g eng
090	PN1995.9.S26 $b T8 2001
092	791.4372 $b T9742
049	UPMM
130 0	2001, a space odyssey (Motion picture)
245 10	2001, a space odyssey $h [videorecording] / $c Metro-Goldwyn-Mayer presents a Stanley Kubrick production ; directed and produced by Stanley Kubrick ; screenplay by Stanley Kubrick and Arthur C. Clarke.
246 3	Two thousand and one, a space odyssey
246 3	Two thousand-one, a space odyssey
246 1	$i Title from disc surface: $a Stanley Kubrick's 2001 : $b a space odyssey

250	Digitally restored and remastered ed.
260	Burbank, CA : $b Warner Home Video, $c c2001.
300	1 videodisc (148 min.) : $b sd., col. ; $c 4 3/4 in.
440	0 Stanley Kubrick collection
538	DVD.
546	English or French language soundtrack (5.1 surround) with optional subtitles in English, French, Spanish, and Portuguese ; closed-captioned in English for the hearing impaired.
511 1	Keir Dullea, Gary Lockwood, William Sylvester, Daniel Richter.
508	Editor, Ray Lovejoy ; director of photography, Geoffrey Unsworth ; music, Aram Khatchaturian, Gyèorgy Ligeti, Johann Strauss, Richard Strauss.
500	". . . preserving the 'scope' aspect ratio of its original theatrical exhibition. Enhanced for widescreen TVs"— Container.
500	Originally produced as a motion picture in 1968.
500	Special features include: New 2000 digital master from re-stored elements ; soundtrack newly remastered in Dolby digital 5.1 ; interactive menus ; theatrical trailer ; scene access.
520	A science fiction film which moves from the pre-historic birth of intelligence toward the emergence of man as pure thought somewhere in the future.
521 8	MPAA rating: G.
650	0 Twenty-first century $v Drama.
650	0 Computers $v Drama.
650	0 Space vehicles $v Drama.
650	0 Human-computer interaction $v Drama.
650	0 Science fiction films.
650	0 Feature films.
650	0 Video recordings for the hearing impaired.
700 1	Kubrick, Stanley.
700 1	Clarke, Arthur Charles, $d 1917–
700 1	Dullea, Keir, $d 1936–
700 1	Lockwood, Gary, $d 1937–
710 2	Metro-Goldwyn-Mayer.
710 2	Warner Home Video (Firm)

APPENDIX B: LIBRARY AV WORKFLOW PROCESS INFORMATION REQUIREMENTS

Information Needed	UFO	Cataloging	MediaTech
1. Title	√	√	√
2. Variant Title	Sometimes	√	Sometimes
3. Series Title	Sometimes	√	Sometimes
4. Cross Reference Titles/other versions			Sometimes
5. Subtitles	Sometimes	√	√
6. Subject Fields (from Library of Congress)		√	
7. Keywords (MT list)			√
8. Physical Description—include running time if avail	Sometimes	√	
9. Running Time		√	√
10. Format (DVD/VHS)	√	√	√
11. Color or b/w or both		√	√
12. Sound or Silent		√	√
13. Publisher/Distributor/Year	√	√	√
14. Copyright date		√	√
15. ISBN and Other Standard Numbers	Sometimes	√	√
16. # Pieces	√	√	√
17. Del. Weight			√
18. Actors	Sometimes	√	√
19. Writer	√		√
20. Director	Sometimes	√	√
21. Producer	Sometimes	√	√
22. Summary	Sometimes	√	√
23. Annotations			√
24. Loc code/area			√
25. Public Performance Rights	√	√	√
26. Purchase Price	√		√
27. Vendor Code	√		√
28. Vendor Name	√		√
29. Vendor Address	√		√
30. Rental Price			√
31. Edition		√	Sometimes
32. Sort Title			√
33. Audience Level			√
34. Language	√	√	√
35. Internal Notes (initials ordering person, notify, need by)	√		√
36. Home Location	√	√	
37. Purchase Order #	√		

Information Needed	UFO	Cataloging	MediaTech
38. Shipping and billing address	√		
39. Link to bib record	√	√	
40. Instructions to Vendor (PPR phrase, need by, discount)	√		√
41. RUSH (within order and on bib for tracking)	√	√	√
42. Selector's order blurb (could be OCLC record)	√		√
43. Physical Inspection	√	√	√
44. Electronic Inspection			√

Note: 44 total items of information/actions needed. 71% needed by more than one area, 16 needed by all three areas (35.5%), 16 needed by two of the three areas (35.5%), 12 needed by one area.

APPENDIX C: PENN STATE UNIVERSITY LIBRARIES AV WORKFLOW PROCESS

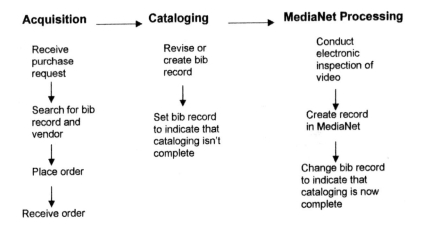

Acquisition ⟶ **Cataloging** ⟶ **MediaNet Processing**

Receive purchase request
↓
Search for bib record and vendor
↓
Place order
↓
Receive order

Revise or create bib record
↓
Set bib record to indicate that cataloging isn't complete

Conduct electronic inspection of video
↓
Create record in MediaNet
↓
Change bib record to indicate that cataloging is now complete

NOTES

1. Marsha Starr Paiste, "Defining and Achieving Quality in Cataloging in Academic Libraries," *Library Collection, Acquisitions, and Technical Services* 27 (2003): 327–338.

2. Jeannette Ho, "Cataloging Practices and Access Methods for Videos at ARL and Public Libraries," *Library Resources and Technical Services* 48, no. 2 (2004): 107–121.

3. Marie L. Bednar, Roger Brisson, and Judy Hewes, "Pursuing the Three Ts: How Total Quality Management, Technology, and Teams Transformed the Cataloging Department at Penn State," *Cataloging and Classification Quarterly* 30, nos. 2/3 (2000): 241–279.

4. Robert B. Freeborn and Rebecca L. Mugridge, "The Reorganization of Monographic Cataloging Processes at Penn State University Libraries," *Library Collections, Acquisitions, and Technical Services* 26 (2002): 35–45.

5. Ann Dodd, Maury Cotter, Lesley Clark, and Ian Hau, "Improving Improvement: Change Strategies in Higher Education" (paper presented at the annual meeting of the National Consortium for Continuous Improvement, New York, July 2001).

6. Ian Hau and Ford Calhoun, *Fast Cycle Change in Knowledge-Based Organizations: Building Fundamental Capability for Implementing Strategic Transformation* (report no. 161) (Madison: University of Wisconsin Center for Quality and Productivity Improvement, 1997).

7. Peter R. Scholtes, Brian L. Joiner, and Barbara J. Streibel, *The Team Handbook*, 3rd ed. (Madison, WI: Oriel, 2003).

8. Scholtes, Joiner, and Streibel, *The Team Handbook*.

9. Dennis S. Gouran, "Communication Skills for Group Decision Making," in *Handbook of Communication and Social Interaction Skills*, ed. John O. Greene and Brant R. Burleson (Mahwah, NJ: Lawrence Erlbaum, 2003), 835–870.

10. Sunwolf and David R. Seibold, "The Impact of Formal Procedures on Group Processes, Members, and Task Outcomes," in *The Handbook of Group Communication Theory and Research*, ed. Lawrence R. Frey, Dennis S. Gouran, and Marshall Scott Poole (Thousand Oaks, CA: Sage, 1999), 395–431.

11. Michael A. West and Giles Hirst, "Cooperation and Teamwork for Innovation," in *International Handbook of Organizational Teamwork and Cooperative Working*, ed. Michael A. West, Dean Tjoswold, and Ken G. Smith (West Sussex, England: John Wiley & Sons, 2003), 297–319.

Chapter 12

Matrix Teams: Advancing Transitions

Michele J. Crump

This chapter discusses matrix management structures and identifies benefits and shortcomings of matrix teams in the academic library environment. The chapter evaluates relevant issues that influence the need for organizational change, such as electronic and digital information, unstable budgets, and patrons' expectations. Applications of matrix teams in several academic libraries show the flexibility this model promotes for responding to future changes in technical services.

Developments in information technology and communication media effect change in the academic library environment almost on a daily basis. Libraries operate in a constant state of transition, acquiring and making available current information in a variety of formats and presentations. Patrons' growing interest in materials published electronically has spurred the growth of electronic and digital collections. Online library catalogs and web presentation of collections have become more efficient and at the same time more complicated and multifaceted. Growth in technology and interest in the products of that development have converged to change the view of the library and in turn have compelled librarians to reconsider their roles and the services the library provides. Remaining attentive to these transitions is a commitment the library organization must make to continue serving all generations of researchers effectively.

Within the organization, matrix management structures offer the flexibility and collaboration that help librarians meet service expectations and responsibilities. This chapter examines matrix structures as a model for assembling staff from technical services and throughout the library system specifically for advancing user-based services. Through example case studies, the chapter considers the current library environment and examines matrix models at work in academic libraries. The discussion outlines the interdependent and interdivisional makeup of matrix structures, relates the expertise matrix teams impart to the library system, and details how such teams serve the necessary role as transition agents and advancers of the library mission.

CURRENT LIBRARY ENVIRONMENT

The current library environment mirrors many of the successes libraries have had in promoting agendas made possible by the growth in information technology. Distance and lifelong learning are products of electronic resources development, which has enlarged services and opened access to information beyond the library building. Increasingly, patrons expect around-the-clock access to the collections. If access is not readily available, patrons expect a librarian to be there 24/7, physically or virtually, to help them locate the material they need. Often unstable budgets coincide with downsizing of units and staff. None of this is news to technical service librarians and paraprofessionals. These circumstances coupled with technological changes create an environment in need of collaborative relationships between all functional divisions in the library.

The 2003 OCLC Environmental Scan: Pattern Recognition is an invaluable report that describes current social, economic, and technology landscapes and offers advice on how libraries should respond to these environmental influences. Through an identification of major trends in the landscape, the report points out patterns that librarians should be aware of in areas such as staffing issues, service roles, users' desires, treatment of content, preservation issues, and budgets.[1] The report suggests that libraries should create opportunities for engaging patrons in mutual dialogue concerning services and the library's presentation of those services. In the past, libraries concentrated on building collections, rather than operating user-centered services. The report acknowledges librarians moving toward collaborative relationships in their organizations and suggests that they expand that practice to form partnerships with the people they serve to remain a key component of the educational landscape—"sustainability is only possible through collaboration."[2]

COLLABORATION THROUGH MATRIX STRUCTURES

Library literature is replete with articles discussing change and offering advice about how organizations should redesign their management structure to better prepare for the future. Preparing for and performing the analysis process for reorganizing has been productive for staff on a number of levels. The redesign methodology gives staff a common language for talking about change and a shared experience that helps them commit to the new structure. Thomas Shaughnessy, in his discussion about reorganization of the University of Minnesota Library System, observed that staff were developing new management skills while participating in these methods, but more importantly, "new attitudes and behaviors were being incubated."[3] This observation points out the benefit of open, democratic organizational structures—the more humane the process, the more the staff will be receptive and "accountable for the well-being of the entire library system."[4] That is why any new management structure should not be a directive from administrators. Wisely, the trend in library management in recent years has been to instill ideas of change in staff through an evaluation and planning period, which outlines redesign methods.

Maureen Sullivan emphasizes this point as she reviews models of organizational development (OD) management techniques that library organizations might apply in effecting deliberate change. Strategic planning, Sullivan stresses, will address the "challenge of creating organizations that are dynamic, customer-focused, relevant, flexible, and prepared for continual change."[5] She reminds the reader of the importance of including staff, both professional and paraprofessional, in every step of the planning process. In that way, future goals are specific to the library and "engage the minds and hearts of staff in a process of meaningful and sustainable change."[6] Planning an organization that can deal with ongoing change and including staff in that process gives everyone in the organization a sense of authority about their part in the work of the library. If carried out and followed up on effectively, the process becomes a growth experience that leads to an organization's continued success.

Strategic planning opens the door to team building and collaboration, thus introducing the matrix structure. In her thorough 1991 article on matrix management, Peggy Johnson explores organizational options and makes a convincing argument "for creating individualized, adaptive structures" in libraries through matrix management.[7] Johnson characterizes matrix management structure as flexible and goal-centric. Within the structure, staff gains independence from chain of command management through cross-functional teams, which form a number of reporting relationships and build teamwork based on shared goals. These cross-functional teams may cut across departments or divisions, and the team members may have multiple supervisors, project managers, and home-base managers. In most cases, well-defined management roles should resolve any problems resulting from multiple reporting lines. Moreover, the benefits far outweigh the negative aspects. Such transitional structures draw on expertise from their members to form goal-oriented groups and execute innovative initiatives for the good of the whole system.[8]

Suzan McGinnis and Jan H. Kemp describe using cross-functional teams to form an electronic resources group at the Texas Tech Library. The team originated with six staff members from four functional areas (information services, bibliographical services, acquisitions, and reference) charged with coordinating the management of electronic resources. McGinnis and Kemp point out the advantage of not having to dismantle the functional departments in place to implement this group. In addition, the group assists communication between departments and units while building the strength of the organization as involved staff expand their knowledge and skills with electronic resources. The authors note that loyalty to the group and their departments could create conflicts, particularly when the team makes decisions that could be seen as self-serving and inattentive to library-wide goals. However, clear directives and communication from departments offering workflow procedures should reduce the occurrence of such conflicts.[9]

Michael Goold and Andrew Campbell maintain that matrix structures require clarity in outlining the team's roles and responsibilities. The responsibilities must be wide-ranging so that the team has guidance but is free to work out the finer points of the plan and procedures for completing a project. Working relationships with other units, "reporting and lateral relationships," should be mapped out to establish certain lines of communication. Each team will understand how its work will be assessed through defined core accountabilities and acknowledge the mutually dependent relationships with other teams in obtaining definite goals. The authors advocate an organizational structure that gives form to the team but also offers validity to working toward creating an environment that welcomes creativity, encourages job satisfaction, and provides a means for achieving "the best collective way forward."[10]

MATRIX STRUCTURE AT WORK

Technical Services Reorganization

Technical Services in the University of Illinois, Chicago, library underwent a redesign of the Catalog and Acquisitions Departments beginning in 1993. The primary reason for the transition was to structure functions in the departments to prepare for the changes in the library environment. Alex Bloss and Don Lanier discuss the development of two matrix teams formed from staff in technical services and headed by librarians from other divisions in the library. These two groups were charged with evaluating workflow and procedures and proposing alternatives. The authors note how the modification of the department heads' authority role changed as staff began performing procedures that they used to manage. Their roles became more refined and humane in that they were guiding, coordinating, monitoring, negotiating, and serving as visionaries in sharing changes in the environment. In this example, matrix organization was employed with a set goal to redesign two departments and promote collaboration and flexibility. Bloss and Lanier ask the question, "Is it possible for hierarchical and team management to continue to coexist?"[11] Their analysis of the changing role of the department head in the library system explains that movement to more of a matrix structure in which teams provide the concepts and direction of the work will mean a flatter structure with more lateral reporting lines.

Bloss and Lanier reported their analysis in late 1997 and at that time indicated that this was the beginning of a system-wide organization redesign. An examination of the University of Illinois, Chicago's library staff website shows clearly that the library coordinates all its systems activities led by an interdivisional matrix contingent, the library Steering Committee. Five quadrants with additional task forces direct the functional areas that incorporate traditional and transitional charges: Collections Management, Electronic Collections, Electronic Resources, Processing and Delivery, and User Services. The direction of this library is to develop programs that respond to or anticipate users' needs. These collegial teams guide the daily work and remain attentive to "emerging issues and the library's response to them."[12]

Library System Reorganization

Eric C. Shoaf reports on the strategic planning approach Brown University Library employed beginning in 1997 to promote change through a major redesign of the organization. The Brown Library used this organizational tool proactively, better positioning their institution for "quantifying and objectifying the library's goals and mission, its values, and its vision for the future."[13] Shoaf explains the fifteen-month planning process that began with a study of the library and staff, resulting in a directive document that recommended cross-section staffing of the steering committee, which developed the strategies that would direct the library's future. One significant observation is that educating the group in strategic plan practices and building camaraderie in the group take time and must not be forced or rushed if the team is to be successful.[14]

Brown Library has moved forward with their library-wide strategic planning, designing a matrix structure that promotes a collaborative organization rather than a hierarchy framework. A virtual visit to Brown Library reveals a well-documented reorganization process, from early strategic planning training through the development of the collaborative groups performing functions that focus "on what our users do: teach, learn, research, publish, access and retrieve resources." The upper management structure has been flattened significantly with the formation of a Coordinator group that advances the goals and vision of the functional groups with that of the library.[15]

Digital Library Development

Duke University Libraries formed a task force to investigate the "programmatic and organizational elements" for forming a digital library. The organizational structure formed to build the digital library consists of three departments under a newly formed division, Information Technology Services. The library substructure relies on matrix management as the three departments, Information Systems Support, Web Services, and Research and Content Development, form an allied workforce "on evolving set products and outcomes intended cumulatively to give programmatic focus to the digital library."[16] In addition to this joint effort, the digital initiatives depend on teams and task forces throughout the libraries and the university to identify and build projects for digitizing and adding to the collection. This example of strategic planning and collaborative effort demonstrates how forward thinking and matrix management can be applied to create a new division within the library that responds to users' desires and the community's archival needs.

Library Initiatives

In a similar fashion, the University of Florida Library's Technology Services division is using matrix structures in building and maintaining several initiatives that are central to the library's strategic plan. The primary functions in the library are organized under four hierarchical divisions: Collection Management, Public Services, Support Services, and Technology Services. The Technology Services committees in almost all cases have professional and/or support staff members from departments in each division. These initiative groups span the divisions, bringing staff together from various work areas to make library-wide proposals, set policies, and foster innovation.

As discussed in earlier examples, matrix management is often used to coordinate teams from cross-departments for a finite project. Library West, one of the libraries in the University of Florida's system, is currently undergoing renovation. To accommodate this upgrade, the humanities and social sciences collections housed in this library were put into storage. The directors of Technology Service, Public Services, and Collection Management appointed a team of librarians from the three divisions to plan and implement the Dewey reclassification of that collection.[17] The team must work with the material in storage and identify what needs to be reclassified and which titles should remain in storage or should be returned to the library once the renovation of that facility is completed. The work of this collaborative group supports a key objective in the University of Florida Library's strategic plan by improving the physical access to the collections. Progress and timeline updates are reported periodically to the three divisional directors.

Two University of Florida Library web committees bring together representatives from the three divisions to set policy and standards for the library's web pages. On an ongoing basis, the Web Advisory Policy Group monitors the creation of pages and liaisons with the university's web policy administration, which sets the style sheet for the official look of the complete University of Florida website.[18] The recently formed Resource Navigation Task Force is a library-wide team charged with improving navigation of the libraries' website.[19] Application of the group's findings should result in effortless navigation for users searching databases, electronic journals and books, and digitized materials. Librarians from Public Services and Technology Services chair the team collaboratively, offering guidance from the technical and users' point of view. Like the Web Advisory Group, this task force team draws its members from the three divisions but reports their progress to the director of Technology Services. The work of these two matrix teams supports the library's strategic objective to improve access to information resources for the campus community.

The University of Florida's Digital Library Center was formed from select staff out of Preservation, Collection Development, and newly created support positions. The Center draws support from two technical services areas, the Cataloging and Metadata Department for indexing expertise to make the digitized material accessible and the Systems Department for improving and maintaining the systems and networks the Center utilizes. The Digitized Collection Advisory Group, a team in the planning stages, will be a consultative cross-functional team made up of staff from throughout the three divisions to offer public service, access, network and system, and collection development information and applications. The advisor group will be charged with identifying collections within the libraries, on campus, and from the community at large. Concurrently, the Center will continue identifying digital initiatives that will enhance the overall collection and fulfill the library's strategic objective to provide access to storage materials and improve access to information resources for the campus community.

CONCLUSION

In this chapter, I have examined the matrix structure as a management system that allows an organization to better contend with change, particularly within technical services. Technical services are function driven and by their very nature must coordinate workflow with units all through the system. Matrix structures offer flexibility and form at the same time, which makes them an ideal framework for initiating change within an organization, especially in technical services. Collaborative working relationships can be shaped and overlaid on traditional organizations for sharing expertise in launching library-wide objectives. Moreover, exposures to evaluation tools and strategic planning sessions provide excellent staff development opportunities for improving skills and introduce the potential for job satisfaction. Whether employed in a department, in a division, or library-wide, matrix teams help flatten the hierarchical organization by alleviating the management burden in the library through building consensus decision making and innovative problem solving. Collaborative teams as discussed here show how participating in transformative processes will broaden library staff and give them the means for focusing on user-centered objectives.

In the current environment, librarians are embracing change as they are adjusting to it, making the pace of library work very compelling and energizing. We have learned that successful organizations plan proactively for the future. The matrix model, when applied effectively, can humanize library operations and empower library staff to think collegially about managing change and to think creatively about using technology. As we apply what we have learned and engage patrons in conversations about their research needs and usability desires, this alliance will promote the necessary transitions for the library of today and tomorrow.

NOTES

1. Alane Wilson, ed. *The 2003 OCLC Environmental Scan: Pattern Recognition* (Dublin, OH: OCLC Online Computer Library Center, Inc., 2004), 72.

2. Wilson, *The 2003 OCLC Environmental Scan*, 69.

3. Thomas W. Shaughnessy, "Lessons from Restructuring the Library," *The Journal of Academic Librarianship* 22 (July 1996): 253.

4. Shaughnessy, "Lessons from Restructuring the Library," 254.

5. Maureen Sullivan, "Organization Development in Libraries," *Library Administration and Management* 18, no. 4 (Fall 2004): 179.

6. Sullivan, "Organization Development in Libraries," 183.

7. Margaret Ann Johnson, "Matrix Management: An Organizational Alternative for Libraries," *The Journal of Academic Librarianship* 16 (September 1990): 224.

8. Johnson, "Matrix Management," 225–228.

9. Suzan McGinnis and Jan H. Kemp, "The Electric Resources Group: Using the Cross-Functional Team Approach to the Challenge of Acquiring Electronic Resources," *Library Acquisitions: Practice and Theory* 22, no. 3 (1998): 297–299.

10. Michael Goold and Andrew Campbell, "Making Matrix Structures Work: Creating Clarity on Unit Roles and Responsibility," *European Management Journal* 21, no. 3 (2003): 351–360.

11. Alex Bloss and Don Lanier, "The Library Department Head in the Context of Matrix Management and Reengineering," *College and Research Libraries* 58 (November 1997): 499–508.

12. University of Illinois, Chicago, Library, "Library Interdepartmental Committees, Quadrants, Task Forces," September 15, 2004, www.uic.edu/depts/lib/staff/QuadsComsTFs04.pdf (accessed October 21, 2004).

13. Eric C. Shoaf, "Fifteen Months in the Planning Trenches: Strategically Positioning the Research Library for a New Century," *Library Administration and Management* 15, no. 1 (Winter 2001): 4.

14. Shoaf, "Fifteen Months in the Planning Trenches," 11.

15. Brown University Library, "A User-Centered Design for a New Organizational Framework Design Evolution & Cultural Thinking," May 2002, www.brown.edu/Facilities/University_Library/MODEL/LTMG/neworg/ (accessed August 5, 2004).

16. Paul Conway, "Deep Infrastructure Supports Digital Library Services," *Syllabus*, May 1, 2004, http://syllabus.com/print.asp?ID=9362 (accessed August 16, 2004).

17. University of Florida Library, Technology Services Division, "Library West Collection Preparation Committee," August 10, 2004, http://web.uflib.ufl.edu/ts/lw%20collprep2.htm (accessed February 14, 2005).

18. University of Florida Library, Technology Services Division, "Web Advisory Group," November 4, 2004, http://web.uflib.ufl.edu/wag/ (accessed February 14, 2005).

19. University of Florida Library, Technology Services Division, "Resource Navigation Task Force," January 24, 2005, http://web.uflib.ufl.edu/ts/ResNav%20Charge2.htm (accessed January 25, 2005).

About the Editors
and Contributors

Robert Alan was appointed head of Serials and Acquisitions Services in 2004 after serving as head of the Serials Department (2000–2004) at the Pennsylvania State University. He held previous positions at the University of California, Davis, and the University of California, San Diego, and has worked extensively in the areas of serials cataloging, acquisitions, and preservation. Mr. Alan received his MLS from the University of Arizona.

M. Sue Baughman is the assistant dean for Organizational Development at the University of Maryland (UM) Libraries, a position held since 2000. Prior to this, she was the manager of Public Services in the McKeldin Library at UM. She has held leadership positions at the Essex-Hudson Regional Library Cooperative (NJ), the Maryland State Department of Education, Division of Library Development and Services, and the Anne Arundel County Public Library (MD).

Rosann Bazirjian came to the University of North Carolina at Greensboro in 2004 as university librarian from the Pennsylvania State University, where she served as assistant dean for Technical and Access Services since 1999. In this position she was responsible for all aspects of library access (including interlibrary loan, lending, disability services, and reserves), acquisitions, business operations, and cataloging. She previously held positions at Florida State University, Syracuse University, and the University of West Florida. She is a former member of the PALINET Board of Trustees and the OCLC Members Council and has served on committees and task forces of several professional library organizations. The author of 28 articles, chapters, and reviews, Bazirjian has coedited four volumes of the annual Charleston Conference Proceedings. In July 2005, she became president of the Association for Library Collections and Technical Services, a division of the American Library Association.

Bazirjian received her bachelor's degree from the Herbert H. Lehman College of the City University of New York, a master of science in library service from Columbia University, and a master of social science from the Maxwell School of Public Administration at Syracuse University.

Eleanor I. Cook is serials coordinator and professor at Appalachian State University, where she has worked for fifteen years. She is chief editor of ACQNET-L and has served in leadership positions within a number of professional organizations such as ALA ALCTS, the North American Serials Interest Group, and the North Carolina Library Association.

Michele J. Crump is the chair of the Acquisitions and Licensing Department at the University of Florida Libraries. She has worked in the library's Technical Services division since 1991 and in her current position oversees processing units for payment, monograph acquisitions, serials and electronic resources acquisitions, and gifts and exchange. Prior to returning to her home state of Florida, Michele worked as a paraprofessional for seventeen years in the Serials Department at Stanford University Libraries performing a variety of acquisitions, cataloging, and management assignments. She received her MLIS from San Jose State University while working at Stanford.

Ann H. Dodd is the assistant dean for strategic initiatives in the College of Agricultural Sciences at Penn State University, where her responsibilities include strategic planning, implementation of strategic initiatives, and assessment of program impact. Prior to joining the College of Agricultural Sciences, Ann served for five years as a senior consultant in Penn State's Office of Planning and Institutional Assessment. She joined Penn State in 1999 after five years at the University of North Carolina, Chapel Hill, where she last served as executive assistant to the vice chancellor and director of institutional effectiveness. Her previous employers include the University of Wisconsin, Madison, EXPCT in Madison, Wisconsin, PACE Enterprises in Alexandria, Virginia, and Iowa State University. Ann holds a PhD in communication arts and sciences from Penn State, as well as an MS degree in higher education and a BS degree in family services, both from Iowa State University.

Robert B. Freeborn is the Music/AV cataloging librarian atPennsylvania State University. He previously held the position of nonbook cataloger/preservation librarian at the University of Mississippi and has worked extensively in the areas of music and audiovisual cataloging. Mr. Freeborn received an MM in music history and literature from Kansas State University, and an MLS from Emporia State University.

Stephanie Hartman is the information services librarian of the Engineering and Science Libraries at MIT. Prior to her current position, Stephanie was the Barker Engineering Library processing supervisor for four years, and previous to that spent over five years with the Dewey and Humanities Processing Team. She holds a BA in history from Kenyon College, and a MS in library and information science from Southern Connecticut State University.

Marda L. Johnson holds the position of team leader, Technical Services and Archival Processing Team, at the University of Arizona Library. She also chairs the UA's Information Resources Council, responsible for the allocation of the library's annual information access budget. Her previous experience has included both public and academic library work. Ms. Johnson's most recent employment, prior to coming to Arizona, was as an employee of OCLC from 1979 to 1999.

Megan Johnson is the web services librarian at Appalachian State University, where she has worked for one year. It is her first experience working in a team-based environment. Ms. Johnson received her MLIS from the University of North Carolina, Greensboro, in 1993 and worked mainly in public libraries.

John Lubans Jr. is visiting professor at the School of Library and Information Sciences, North Carolina Central University, and teaches two graduate courses on management and the academic library. He holds degrees from the University of Michigan (library science) and the University of Houston (public administration). Currently, he writes the "On Managing " column for LAMA's quarterly *Library Administration and Management* journal. Past columns are on his website, www.lubans.org. LAMA honored "On Managing" with a Certificate of Achievement in June 2004.

Mary McLaren is the administrative services librarian, University of Kentucky Libraries. She received her MLS in library science from the University of Pittsburgh. She received her BA in English from the College of Steubenville in Steubenville, Ohio. Mary has worked in public services, technical services, and administrative arenas during the course of her library career. She has been at the University of Kentucky Libraries since 1987.

Jack G. Montgomery earned his MLS at the University of Maryland, College Park, in 1987. As a law librarian, he worked in acquisitions, serials, and collection development in law libraries in Virginia, Ohio, and Missouri. Montgomery made the transition to the general academic library and to Western Kentucky University in September 1998. As collection services coordinator, he supervises the library's collection development program, the library materials acquisitions process, the "Gifts-in-Kind," and book-repair programs. He is currently a member of the American Library Association and the Kentucky Library Association and speaks frequently at professional meetings. Jack is the coauthor of *Conflict Management for Libraries: Strategies for Positive, Productive Workplace* with Eleanor I. Cook. He also is active with and a conference manager for the annual Charleston Conference.

Rebecca Mugridge has been head of Cataloging Services at Pennsylvania State University for 5 years, supervising 6 cataloging teams, including 28 support staff and 8 librarians. Prior to coming to Penn State, she held positions at Yale University, Robert Morris University, and the University of Pittsburgh. Rebecca has a BA in history from Penn State, an MLS from the University of Pittsburgh, and an MBA from Robert Morris University. Her research interests relate to library and technical services management and authority control. Mugridge serves on the ALCTS Budget and Finance Committee,

ALCTS Cataloging and Classification Section's Committee on Education, Training and Recruitment of Catalogers, and the Program for Cooperative Cataloging Policy Committee.

Michael Norman was appointed head of serials cataloging in 2002 at the University of Illinois, Urbana-Champaign, Library. Previously, he had held the position of head of technical services at the Savannah College of Art and Design (1999–2002) and cataloger/humanities collection development librarian at Appalachian State University (1996–1999). Mr. Norman received his MLIS from the University of North Carolina, Greensboro. His areas of research include providing effective access to electronic and digital resources, transitioning technical service departments to deal with the emerging information age, and serials management.

Paul Orkiszewski is the acquisitions coordinator at Appalachian State University. His previous experience includes positions as a collection development coordinator and music librarian. He is currently editor of www.acqweb.org, the web clearinghouse for library acquisitions information.

Elke Piontek-Ma is the current supervisor and team leader of the Dewey and Humanities Processing Team in the MIT Libraries. She has held this position for four years. Prior to becoming the team leader, Elke worked as a serials assistant on the Dewey and Humanities Processing Team in the Dewey Library for two years. Elke has a PhD and MA in Chinese studies from the University of Wurzburg in Germany and an MS in library and information science from Simmons College.

Michael S. Ray was appointed assistant to the dean of libraries in 1997 after serving as director of the University of Arizona Continuous Organizational Renewal program. He holds a PhD from the UA Center for the Study of Higher Education (1999), where his focus was organization and administration. His PhD research regarded the changing task jurisdictions of librarians. His previous position at the university was as manager of Employee Development and Training in the campus Human Resources Department. He works as an organizational development consultant with numerous higher education and professional organizations and is a certified

Managing Organizational Transition, Meyers-Briggs Type Indicator and Constructive Dialogue instructor.

Gordana Ruth is the Original Cataloging Production Group leader at the University of Maryland, College Park, Libraries. She received her MLS from the same institution in 1988. So far, she has spent her whole career at the UM Libraries, first as the Chinese language cataloger and then briefly as the acting head of the Monographs Cataloging Unit.

Sarah L. Shreeves is a visiting assistant professor of library administration and visiting project coordinator for the IMLS Digital Collections and Content project at the University of Illinois, Urbana-Champaign (UIUC). Prior to UIUC, Sarah worked for nine years (six as part of the Dewey and Humanities Processing Team) in the MIT Libraries in Cambridge, Massachusetts. She holds a BA in medieval studies from Bryn Mawr College, an MA in children's literature from Simmons College, and an MS in library and information science from UIUC.

Janet L. Siar earned her MLS at the University of Maryland, College Park, in 1988. She has worked in acquisitions for twenty-six years as a paraprofessional and professional librarian. She began her professional career as special processes librarian at the University of Maryland in 1998. In 2001, she served as interim head of Acquisitions and became head of Acquisitions in 2004.